CARL S. DUDLEY

COMMUNITY MINISTRY

new challenges, proven steps
to faith-based initiatives

Foreword by James P. Wind

THE
ALBAN
INSTITUTE

The Alban Institute
2121 Cooperative Way, Suite 100
Herndon, VA 20171

Library of Congress Catalog Card Number 2001094871

ISBN 1-56699-256-7

CONTENTS

FACT-Based Figures
for Community Ministries*

*from *FAith Community Today (FACT), A Report on Religion in the United States Today*, Carl S. Dudley and David A. Roozen, Hartford Seminary, 2001.

ACKNOWLEDGMENTS

Mixed with my positive and challenging memories from so many people who contributed to this book is the dreadful sensation that I am unable to mention everyone who provided significant insights along the way. At the core is my appreciation to leaders of 63 congregations and faith-based ministries who shared extensively in our studies, and who are quoted much too briefly. I hope that they will find my composite profile of ministry as compelling as our research team found their powerful stories of faith in action.

In particular, Dirk J. Hart has been a collaborator at many points, especially the implementation through checklists and Web resources. J. Martin Bailey, Trey Hammond, and Harold Dean Trulear shared their extensive professional experience to shape important new dimensions of community ministries. Steve Blackburn, Paul Christie, Rebecca Dudley, and Sue Sporte contributed their knowledge of resources, project critique and personal encouragement. Shirley Dudley and Adair Lummis provided most of the initial interviews in the Hartford area. From other colleagues at Hartford Institute for Religion Research, David Roozen developed the statistical support from FACT data, and Mary Jane Ross reconstructed the text from innumerable near disasters. At Alban, Beth Ann Gaede has, as always, provided excellent oversight and perceptive suggestions for the project. Finally, we would not have been able to contact so many or assemble so much information without the support of the Lilly Endowment in Indianapolis, and the Program for Non-Profit Organizations located at Yale University, whose support was also made possible by the Lilly Endowment.

Faith-Based Community Ministries is not a finished story, but a journey with a long history that continues into the future. My thanks to all who have contributed to this snapshot along the way. It is a picture of beautiful people who, by faith, have a unique impact on the world as they pass through. Thank God.

FOREWORD

More than a decade ago, the Alban Institute published *Basic Steps Toward Community Ministry* by Carl Dudley. The book was sorely needed. Social (or better, human) needs at the local, national, and international levels were increasing and becoming ever more complex. America's homeless population, for example, had grown, as many people with acute mental illness were deinstitutionalized. The need for day care—for both children and seniors—was growing, as fewer spouses stayed home to provide care that traditionally took place within the family. Major public health issues, ranging from our many serious forms of addiction, to infectious diseases such as HIV/AIDS, to our growing national obesity, put new pressures on already overtaxed public health systems. Our prison populations were expanding at such a rate that we were scrambling nationwide to build new institutions to contain the growing number of prisoners. Violence appeared in many forms—from headline-grabbing and horrendous crimes to the even more numerous but hidden forms of sexual, spousal, child, and elder abuse.

Carl Dudley believed back then—and the Alban Institute did, too—that congregations had a pivotal role in addressing these basic human and societal needs. More than believing that congregations should make a difference, he—and we—believed that they could make a difference but often lacked resources to do so. *Basic Steps* attempted to address that situation.

During the decade that has passed since the book appeared, epochal shifts have reinforced the conviction that congregations must make a greater difference in our world. These shifts in our society, however, have also made it even more difficult for congregations to make that difference. Consider just a few turning points. In 1996 the U.S. Congress passed legislation that "ended welfare as we know it." A key element in that legislation was a provision establishing "charitable choice" as a new framework for helping congregations and other faith-based organizations make use of governmental funding.

These changes were truly epochal. The welfare state built up from the days of Franklin Roosevelt's presidency was dismantled. A new word, *devolution*, entered our vocabulary, as we watched layers of federal programming designed to meet social needs unravel. Suddenly, congregations and other faith-based organizations found themselves in the spotlight. President William Clinton called on congregations to help people find jobs. Other public figures argued that religious institutions could solve problems that government and modern philanthropy had failed to adequately address. Still others worried that this change was a colossal mistake that would leave many in an even greater crisis than the welfare system had. Many people suspected that devolution was an attempt by a conservative Congress to shift from government to religious institutions the burden of caring for those most in need. As he assumed office, President George W. Bush made it clear that he also expected more of congregations and that he intended to create an initiative that would make it possible for faith-based organizations of many kinds to have access to public funds and play new roles in our national life.

Many of us have been concerned that a romanticism is at work here about congregations and other faith-based not-for-profits. Most of these organizations are small and have meager programs. How could such a congregation become a partner with a local or state government when in many cases these institutions have no experience managing grants, minimal budgeting experience, and virtually no staff time to invest in such efforts? But times have changed. The safety net of the welfare system is gone. Charitable choice remains the law of the land, and it stands as a challenge to congregations to do more, although its meaning for American religion remains a mystery.

These changes in the welfare system of our country were not the only seismic shifts we have seen in the past decade. The mighty stock market roared and then whined. The gap between rich and poor—both at home and around the world—has widened. The global environment has become more fragile. HIV/AIDS rages across Africa and Asia. And civilizations clash at regional flash points such as Israel and Bosnia and within our own borders. The terrorist attacks of September 11, 2001, made it apparent that our world is at risk. As thousands flocked to congregations in the days following the attacks, they called out to congregations to make a difference in a world that is dangerous and in trouble.

Carl Dudley has devoted his entire career to addressing this challenge. On the one hand, as a researcher and leader of the congregational studies movement, Dudley has tried to help all of us understand that congregations are much more and do much more that most of us recognize. On the other hand, as a pastor and seminary professor, he has tried to equip pastors and congregational leaders to lead their churches and synagogues into new social ministries. Those who know Dudley know of the deep passion and conviction that motivates him. He believes that God calls congregations to minister to people at their points of deepest need. Period. We also know of his energy. Dudley has directed two of the largest research efforts into congregational life ever mounted, one (at McCormick Seminary) that studied the process of starting new community ministries and another (at Hartford Seminary) that assembled more information on congregational life from more denominations than had ever been attempted before.

The fruits of all this effort are apparent in the pages that follow. Here are steps to help congregations develop new community ministries—and actual instruments and processes that can be used to help congregations make the move from vague intentions to specific actions. Here are examples of various types of social ministry and testimonies from people who have shaped them. As you read ahead, expect frank talk about the new challenges we face. Community ministry requires congregations to do things that they do not know how to do—raise money beyond the normal stewardship framework, partner with other religious and secular groups, employ and supervise staff, create new institutional forms (faith-based not-for-profits) to work in this new environment. These are complicated and risky undertakings. Mistakes will be made. In one telling anecdote—watch for it!—Dudley tells of a community ministry that applied for a $10,000 grant and discovered later that it had cost $75,000 in other resources to complete the task.

Clearly, the world needs more from our congregations; but that is not the whole story. Dudley believes, as I do, that by grappling with the needs of our local and global communities, congregations have the opportunity to discern their true callings. In these ministries, people are given the chance to let their better selves emerge. In the encounters with strangers and neighbors through these ministries comes a spiritual experience, a sense of participating in God's loving of the world. So Dudley invites us to step up to the challenges of this new and dangerous time. He calls on us to let new realities like charitable choice push "all congregations to ask the right questions, to reconsider their priorities, and to imagine new possibilities" (page173).

JAMES P. WIND, PRESIDENT
THE ALBAN INSTITUTE

Faith-Based Community Ministries in a 9/11 World

Dial 9-1-1 in an emergency! Nine eleven has new meaning burned into citizen consciousness following the terrorist attacks on the United States on September 11, 2001.[1] "Emergency conditions" continue for people of this nation and in other countries throughout the world. Among its countless consequences, even after time has passed, this event continues to pose a profoundly religious challenge that finds expression from the individual psyche to broad national policies and international relations. It increases the need for faith-based ministries of compassion and justice, while it influences every aspect of organizing and supporting these programs through religious communities.

Religious responses to the attack were immediate and virtually universal: Impromptu religious shrines were erected; spontaneous worship events occurred in public places along with hastily scheduled traditional liturgies in established sanctuaries. News media provided religious images and interpretations, and seasoned reporters offered theological reflection on the meaning of these events. On the weekend after the attack, attendance burgeoned at all sorts of religious gatherings of worshipers who mourned the suffering and loss of life. Religious leaders raised and responded to questions of meaning, and provided much-needed spiritual reassurance for a confused nation.

Historically in most neighborhoods, churches and synagogues have attempted to help people get through hard times, especially those caused by sudden emergencies. The community ministries that churches most frequently mention are those that address crises with emergency money, food, clothing, shelter, medical attention, and personal counseling. As seen in information from the study of Faith Communities Today (FACT),[2] religious congregations see themselves as the "safety net" for neighbors in need, offering the basics: money, food, clothing, counseling and medical care.

Figure 1.
Five Most Frequent Community Ministries
in Faith Communities Today

Five areas of most frequent response: % YES

Cash assistance to families or individuals.............................. 88%
Food pantry or soup kitchen... 85%
Thrift shop / clothing closet... 61%
Counseling or crisis "hotline"... 46%
Hospital and nursing home.. 45%

Faith Communities Today (FACT) A Report on Religion in the United States Today, 2001

The magnitude of the September 11 attacks overwhelmed existing emergency systems beyond the resources of churches, hospitals, and state agencies combined. In the aftermath, religious bodies are more challenged to respond to the continuing injury to the psyche and soul of Americans. More than a natural disaster (like an earthquake or storm), this attack destroyed the myth of American invulnerability, and was more difficult to "explain." Some literally in shock, citizens absorbed the reality that we had been attacked within our borders. Like all others, our nation is vulnerable.

The stress akin to combat fatigue, previously known only on foreign soil, has become a domestic, personal, and continuing experience. Subsequent terrorist incidents involving anthrax from unknown sources have further destabilized assumptions of personal security. These threats are aimed not only at highly visible leaders but also at postal workers and other ordinary citizens. Americans show the physical, psychological, and spiritual symptoms of stress. This stress is a medical and public health issue, and it is a significant faith-challenge to religious leaders as well. This chronic crisis creates a new context for all social ministries.

INCREASED NEED

Although the context has changed, the need for a wide variety of community ministries has increased; at the same time our national resources for responding to crises have diminished. Americans have been extraordinarily generous in an outpouring of financial support to agencies offering direct assistance to families and individuals who have suffered loss and injury. But in the process, we have seen a significant reduction in available funding for many other philanthropic programs.

Caught in a trough of nongiving that has followed the massive generosity in response to September 11 attacks, local charities across the country are suffering a stunning loss. From soup kitchens to symphonies, from AIDS programs to animal shelters, from museums to medical research, a decline has occurred in anticipated financial support for local support, according to news stories from every part of the country. Only a rally among a few giants softens the blow. Writing in the *San Francisco Chronicle*, Carolyn Said captured the essence:

> The culprit for the "perfect storm" scenario of increased need and decreased donations is already well known: The existing economic downturn, which was accelerated in sectors such as tourism and aviation by the Sept. 11 terrorist attacks, has led to a huge spike in joblessness. At the same time, people who are feeling the pinch are donating less to charities—or contributing to relief efforts instead of giving to local groups.[3]

Some large campaigns and crisis-related organizations (like the American Red Cross and the Salvation Army) have maintained their "market share," while other more prominent efforts have suffered. In the shadow of this watershed event, faith-based social ministries have been asked to do more with less.

Beyond philanthropic limitations, the general economy has suffered as well. The global conflict with terrorism, unlike mobilization for other wars, has not produced a robust economy at home. Rather, economic disorientation has increased domestic unemployment for some and poverty for others. Although this might have been a time for congregations to expand social ministries, their traditional funding sources are suddenly severely limited. To survive in these difficult conditions, all nonprofit organizations, including community ministries, must be more aggressive in challenging volunteers and more imaginative in their funding their programs.

Fortunately, at the same time the spirit of community sharing has increased. In response to the September 11 attacks we have seen a dramatic increase in the number of people who feel moved to volunteer in community service. Capital Research reports:

> Charities are reporting that volunteerism is up. Robert Goodwin, [p]resident of the Points of Light Foundation in Washington, D.C., says the organization has been flooded with calls from people looking to volunteer. The KeyCorp company reports that 10,000 of its 22,000 employees turned out for the company's volunteer day recently, up from 8,000 last year. . . . Steve Cultertson, president of Youth Service America, is pleased with the surge in volunteerism. "That makes me optimistic that in the long term, philanthropy will flow back into the local communities."[4]

Many volunteers are looking for ways to express their concerns, act out their beliefs, and find meaning in service to and with others. This enactment of faith includes participation in outreach programs that cross differences in race, class, religion, language, culture, and national origin. A wide variety of faith based programs have provided natural expressions for this renewal of caring in communities across our land.

EXPANDED PLURALISM

The working definition of religious diversity in American consciousness has changed forever as a result of the events of September 11. At one time dominated by the public awareness of Christians, Jews, and "others," our public religious pluralism now openly includes Muslims in America. About 2 million Muslims regularly attend worship, suggesting about a 6 million total Muslim population in the United States (if the same proportion attend worship as in other religious bodies). Muslims, although more frequently located in urban areas, now rank numerically about on a par with each of several historic denominations, such as Disciples of Christ, Episcopalians, Jews, and Presbyterians (but significantly less than the largest faith groups of Roman Catholics, Baptists, and Methodists). Although Muslim beliefs (based in the Qur'an) and faith practices (such as head-coverings for women) are different, the social ministries of Muslim congregations are remarkably similar to those of other religious groups in the United States.

According to a study by the Council on American Islamic Relations, using FACT data,[5] for example, Muslim congregations also serve their communities with primary social ministries.

Figure 2.
Five Most Frequent Community Ministries
in Mosques in United States

Five areas of most frequent response: % YES

Cash assistance to families or individuals.............................	90%
Marital or family counseling..	77%
Food pantry or soup kitchen..	69%
Prison or jail program..	66%
Thrift shop/clothing closet..	64%

Council on American-Islamic Relations: *A Report from the Mosque Study Project*

In the high-priority and specific profile of the social ministries they provide, Muslim congregations' work appears similar to the outreach programs found in the churches and synagogues down the street. From these comparable studies of FACT data, we see that Muslim faith communities report a slightly higher level of involvement in all social ministries. The Muslim pattern differs from the total study only in the Muslim emphasis on prison-related social concerns, which receives slightly more stress than the total survey support for medical and health ministries among the five most frequently reported outreach programs. In the FACT data, faith communities of all sorts report high levels of response to community social concerns. It's a premium priority for all religious groups, a natural expression of our faith in action.

BACKGROUND AND CHANGES

Congregations have organized their faith-in-action into social ministries for centuries. Roughly a decade ago I described the step-by-step development of faith-based social ministries in *Basic Steps toward Community Ministry* (Washington: Alban Institute, 1991). The book was based on experiences of teaching teams in Chicago and Peoria, Illinois, and in Indianapolis and Lafayette, Indiana, helping Christian congregations to develop strong, effective community ministries. In the process we engaged 60 churches and parishes to help leaders create 25 faith based community programs of compassion and justice. We worked with a wide variety of congregations—mainline, evangelical, and Catholic churches; located in metropolitan centers, small cities, and rural communities; drawn from Euro-American, African American, Hispanic, and Asian cultures. Most were typical churches—that is, not already heavily involved in social issues but willing to begin or expand a community ministry program. More than a decade later, most of these ministries continue to serve their communities.

WELFARE IN TRANSITION

Like an aerial acrobat swinging from one trapeze to the next, even before September 11, 2001, social welfare programs in the United States were in the midst of a precarious transition. Matched only by the impact of the Great Depression, in the past few years social, religious, economic, and political forces have rewritten the rules for developing ministries in at risk communities in America. From the Oval Office in the White House in Washington, D.C., to literally thousands of little white churches (and synagogues and mosques) across the country, faith based initiatives for community ministries had become more significant, and more controversial, than in any generation since the Great Depression of the 1930s.

The great shift came in the adoption of legislation that promised to move people receiving public assistance "from welfare to work." In 1996 a Republican Congress passed and a Democratic President signed the bill that delivered the message in its title, "Personal Responsibility and Work Opportunity Reconciliation Act." This act, which President Clinton called "the end of welfare as we have known it," provided strong incentives for state agencies to encourage welfare recipients to develop economic self sufficiency. Further, the national legislation demanded that states implement termination dates and lifetime limits for most current welfare recipients.

Because of welfare to work provisions, funding that had once been available through welfare departments was shifted to programs in labor and educational agencies to support employment training, and social case workers were replaced by vocational counselors. The timing of this watershed transition is significant: By September 2001, the majority of former welfare recipients had been guided and pushed into various modes of economic independence. Although the economy had been thriving, these newly trained workers remained particularly vulnerable.

In the year before the September 11 attacks, I had asked the leaders of faith based ministries in my city to assess the transitional situation. In general, they reported that we were in the midst of a major transition. In the process they noted that many welfare recipients were struggling and vulnerable. These are typical responses.[6]

> A very small percentage are doing much better; they are working, and they have an improved sense of their self esteem and are doing well; but there is a bigger percentage of people who are having a worse time than they ever had [*director, soup kitchen*].

> I think the theory that the state can save money by cutting welfare is true. But what is not taken into account is the measurement of the impact, especially on children. You have more and more families doubling up; what is a three bedroom unit becomes a three family unit. A two family house becomes a five family house [*executive, housing agency*].

> We are having more and more parents who are homeless who are coming to the shelter than we have had in the past. . . . People are poorer, poorer than they were before, and they have less money. And then with that money you have to go to work and then you have to pay for day care and transportation costs. So your expenses have gone up and your income has gone down [*manager, temporary family shelter*].

In this new configuration of social welfare, the social ministries of faith communities were among the first to feel the impact of change, and to seek to reach the lives of those caught in the transition. Political forces, seeing the church in the middle, made a second major change in the social-services landscape.

DISCOVERING FAITH-BASED MINISTRIES

Into that tenuous social climate entered George W. Bush with a strong commitment to encourage faith based ministries to take on a larger share of responsibility for encouraging and, it was hoped, transforming the lives of welfare recipients. In the presidential election of 2000 Bush supported the provision in the 1996 Welfare Act known as "charitable choice." This section of the law requires that states using federal funds permit religious organizations to compete and, if successful, to receive funding on the same basis as other nongovernmental agencies—without giving up their religious character. Immediately after his inauguration in January 2001, President Bush made charitable choice a primary initiative for his new administration, including a White House Office and expanded legislative support. As the terrorists attacks hit eight months later, Congress was debating new legislation to expand the use of contracts, vouchers, and other funding for "charitable, religious, or private organizations" to provide services far beyond the initial allocation to Temporary Assistance for Needy Families, Medicaid, Food Stamps and similar programs.

Regardless of the shape of additional legislation, the role of faith based ministries will remain a defining issue for the next several years.

Historically the Salvation Army, Catholic Charities, Lutheran Family Services, Jewish Federation, and other religious agencies have contracted for programs with funding from government agencies. They have worked at local, state, and even federal level with millions of public dollars invested in the programs they provided. "Charitable choice" legislation reaffirmed the value of the work that these religious bodies contributed to the whole society. As models for additional faith based community ministry programs, they underscored the appropriate roles for professionals serving with volunteer caregivers in large and sustainable programs. Over the years they have provided a religious witness without denying the freedom of clients to retain their own very different religious persuasions. But the current debate on charitable choice and faith based ministries goes beyond the practices of these long established social agencies.

EXPANDING AND REDEFINING THE PARTNERS

On a national level, the debates surrounding charitable choice have often heightened tensions produced by differences. Evangelical and liberal Protestants, for example, have differed over the clarity of religious expression permitted as a condition of receiving services, while some conservative Christians have resisted funding programs provided by non-Christian religious groups, or permitting the government to decide what is a legitimate religion.

Although the national rhetoric has focused on differences, local communities seeking charitable-choice funding have bridged some of the bitter divisions. Often they have worked together as siblings within a family of religious groups, not by resolving differences but by accepting them. Local networks of stakeholders (beginning with churches and agencies, but often including schools and businesses) gathered in support of community ministries have a power to renew faith within each group, even as these community programs provide common ground to accept their differences. These ministries have been midwife to fascinating coalitions of black and white; city and suburb; Catholic and Protestant; evangelical and liberal; Christian, Jewish and Muslim. While recognizing our differences, some faith based community ministries provide a deeply satisfying experience of common ground.

This need for additional help in combination with the potential of faith based ministries has produced new, unexpected partners drawn from previously distinct institutional groups of business, philanthropy, education, and religious organizations. New partnerships form as old divisions disappear. Government agencies already work closely with business in concerns for employee health and safety, for example. Business overlaps the public sphere in a wide variety of institutions, from prisons to hospitals to welfare agencies, where "privatization" is a recognized alternative. Philanthropy, education, government, and business often come together for research and product development. Employment agencies may create horizontal links with secular agencies and religious job-training programs. A government sponsored housing development may include private, religious, and commercial interests. Abounding examples of productive collaboration underscore the wide margins of cooperation that already link government with business and philanthropy.

In the context of new and unexpected collaboration throughout the culture, charitable choice is only one of many partnerships in a much larger movement. Because of the uniquely American tradition of the separation of church and state, charitable-choice funding for faith-based social ministries raises unique questions for participants, which we shall explore from various practical perspectives. But in the larger sweep of social changes, it comes at a time of great need when innovative alliances are already being constructed that cross many old institutional differences.

CHALLENGES FOR COMMUNITY MINISTRY

Terrorist attacks of September 11, 2001—momentarily the most dramatic—were only one of several powerful forces that have put faith-based community ministries in the center of a "perfect storm." Collectively these forces include new welfare legislation as interpreted by the president, a national (and worldwide) economic depression and struggle for recovery, and the expanded need for social services for people moving from welfare to work, and for others simply out of work in a transitional and uncertain economy. The implications for faith communities are both harsh and promising:

- Apparent reduction in personal charity and corporate philanthropy donations to most local nonprofit groups, including faith-based ministries.
- In the spirit of community response to crisis, both political and religious efforts to increase the number of volunteers willing to pitch in.
- Additional government funding choice for faith-based ministries announced in legislation such as charitable choice, but competing with government commitments to domestic security and international military activity.
- Continuing political and religious tensions about the appropriate expression of "sectarian beliefs" in programs supported by government funding.
- Expanded interfaith openness toward community ministries that are shared among Christian, Jewish, Muslim, and other faith groups through neighborhood organizations and regional networks.
- Creative coalitions and partner-programs among government, education, commercial, philanthropic, and religious groups.

Our ability to make something positive from these new conditions will depend on many factors that are reflected in this book. These include maximizing leadership and location, and a wise use of history, politics, and resources—physical and spiritual. The leaders we interviewed particularly stressed these three issues that challenge faith-based ministries in this radically new era, namely:

- How should churches, mosques and synagogues respond to a growing demand for social welfare services?

- How should these religious groups respond responsibly to the possibilities of government funding for faith-based ministries while remaining true to their spiritual vocation?
- How can faith communities make the most of new configurations of business, education, philanthropy, and government resources for ministry?

In this time of transition, adaptive congregations can find amazing new resources to develop and expand their social ministries. This book is written to help congregations like yours make the most of these opportunities. Such congregations can renew their commitments and relationships to have an impact on the communities from which they come and in which they are, by God's grace, agents of care, healing, and transformation.

PROVEN STEPS, MANY PATHS

Under these new conditions we have revisited the earlier guidelines for the initial steps in building social ministries—some have continuing vitality, and others need to be revised in light of changing conditions. As the guidelines have evolved, your group needs to address four interdependent choices if it is to build a solid foundation for your ministry. The first is your *social context*—the place and people around your center. While your community context does not determine your ministry, it provides the framework of social forces, lifestyles, and community resources within which your ministry takes place. Second is your *congregational identity*, that unique character of faith, history, and personality that form your culture. Congregational identity reflects the core values and commitments that shape your church and guide its response to the challenges of change. The third is the *organization for ministry* that gives your ministry the capacity to respond to your context in ways consistent with your identity. Fourth are the *partnerships*, the networks of relationship and commitment that broaden the base and give the ministry stability over time.

Therefore, this book is structured around the interplay of context, identity, organization, and partnerships in community ministry. Together these elements are essential to gaining the commitment of any congregation to a community ministry. For your parish to support the ministry, four things need to happen:

- Members of the congregation must see the community as their "turf," their responsibility, and must accept the need for the ministry you target (social context).
- Members must respond to this need as a natural and significant part of their Christian commitment (congregational identity).
- Members must have the managerial capacity to respond to that need in a way that can make a difference in people's lives (organization).
- Members must recognize the larger connections and resources in which your ministry functions (partnerships).

These four elements are interdependent, and in a sense, they must happen at the same time. Most groups, however, choose to concentrate on one aspect at a time.

You need not go through all the steps before you respond to a particularly obvious need for community ministry. From experience, I have listed the essential elements for mobilizing social ministry. These reflect the foundations that are most helpful, but they can be constructed in whatever order seems appropriate. You may wish to begin with a study of identity rather than context, or begin with the study of people rather than boundaries. If you have already begun your ministry, or have been working at it for a long time, these steps may provide a review of what you have done and fresh energy as you continue. By picking and choosing, you may find ways to strengthen your ministry, set it in a larger context, or discover additional resources. I am advocating not a formula for ministry, but a selection of working tools to be used in ways that only you can identify.

To illustrate how the guidelines work, I have collected examples of how church groups have used them. The examples are drawn from reports written by local teams of clergy and lay leaders and from interviews by staff of the Hartford Institute for Religion Research in two areas of the country. The *Church and Community Project* worked with a wide variety of Christian congregations, roughly reflecting the distribution of Christian churches in the Midwest. The *Project on Religion, Welfare, and Politics 2000* included an even more diverse group of socially active churches, synagogues, and faith-based social agencies in New England. In the first project we were concerned primarily with beginning social ministries, and in the second we looked at some changes in faith-based ministry since the passage of the 1996 national welfare legislation. In the Midwest we concentrated on starting new ministries, and in New England we looked at the continuing relationships in the light of new welfare legislation. (For both groups I have provided a thumbnail sketch of participating congregations and faith-based ministries in appendix A.) These passages give voice to the perceptions and commitments of local church leaders who have mobilized their congregations in developing community social ministries.

Think of these examples as snapshots from a congregational family album on ministry. Like photographs, these excerpts highlight particular features, set in the appropriate social context. The value of these examples is not in their similarities, but in the subtle differences that customize generic guidelines to fit the unique character of that particular setting for ministry. Rather than reading them straight through, you may prefer to pick and choose, focusing specifically on those areas that speak directly to your situation. I hope these illustrations will tickle your imagination and that, liberated from the oppression of a foreign formula for planning, you can find your own best way.

Together the guidelines and the examples provide an array of resources for congregational leaders to use in shaping their own ministries without the need for consultants or staff assistance. You will see how others have faced a variety of problems so that you can study more carefully options for dealing with immediately relevant issues. This do-it-yourself approach reaffirms the capacity of typical churches to develop uniquely effective ministries when grown naturally in their own appropriate style.

MOTIVATIONS FOR COMMUNITY MINISTRY

As you examine the guidelines and examples, you will notice that congregations of all sorts can engage in compassionate outreach to help people in need and to transform communities. They may organize and support similar programs, but the ways they explain their ministries are different, unique to their congregation's own character, and compelling to many of its members.

You will also notice that congregations become involved in social ministries for different reasons. Some ministries respond to the needs of families and individuals in their community, some reflect the fear of changes in the church neighborhood, some result from the efforts of a few committed members, and others seek to recruit new church members. Most congregations act from a mixture of motives, but their ministries of concern are virtually always a natural expression of their faith. Typically the motives for these ministries are rooted in a common Judeo-Christian tradition. Jesus began his ministry with these compassionate words from the prophet Isaiah (61:1): "The Spirit of the Lord is upon me, because he has anointed me to preach good news to the poor. He has sent me to proclaim release to the captives and recovery of sight to the blind, to let the oppressed go free, to proclaim the year of the Lord's favor" (Luke 4:18-19).

Christian churches reported their community ministries were established in response to the "great commandment" that Jesus quoted from the Hebrew Scripture (Deut. 6:4 and Lev. 19:18): "You shall love the Lord your God with all your heart, and with all your soul, and with all your mind, and with all your strength . . . and you shall love your neighbor as yourself" (Mark 12:30-31). Christians emphasized their commitments to enact the expectations envisioned in Jesus' parable that we will feed the hungry, clothe the naked, welcome the stranger, and minister to the infirm and imprisoned—remembering the words of Jesus, "Just as you did it to one of the least of these who are members of my family, you did it to me" (Matt. 25:40). For many religious communities, as in a synagogue in our more recent interviews, the act of gathering food has been incorporated into the rituals of worship. "People bring food when they come to Yom Kippur, and all the food we collect is sent to Food Share, the regional food bank. We collect between 17 and 18 thousand pounds of food in a single day."

Whatever a faith community's motivation for ministries of compassion and justice, however, such ministries do not happen until someone cares enough to act. No amount of pressure and no organizational procedure can make someone love another enough to step forward and help. Pain, hardship, loss, and sadness are often triggers for sensitive believers. Sometimes we worry about our own conditions, and that concern expands to include others as well. When poverty wears a child's face, when a friend is unemployed, when the children or the elderly or the broken families are real to us—then, by the strange power of God's Spirit, their pain may trigger the necessary energy and endurance in us to organize a ministry in response. As one church member discovered, "It hurts more when you know their names."

Social ministry begins with one or two individuals who care, but they must gather others who share their hopes for touching individuals, changing systems, and empowering people. This act of faith provides the foundation and sustaining energy for building a new ministry. The group may be official or informal; it may be homogeneous or diverse; it may focus on a specific ministry or share a wider concern for the welfare of the community—but the members of this group must be willing to make the development of this ministry a priority in their lives. In short, you need a group—task force, alliance, collective, committee—that feels God's call to take up this cause. That action group is the basis of your new or renewed ministry.

READING THIS BOOK

As you read this book, I recommend that you approach it as a kind of dialogue between prescription and description, between the general statement of what might be done and glimpses of what particular congregations and agencies *have* done. These examples offer windows through which we can see a variety of groups in action, planning and doing social ministries.

I also recommend that you pay close attention to the resources mentioned throughout the book. The past decade has witnessed a dramatic mingling of spiritual and social concerns, as if the socially sensitive liberal churches recognized their need for explicit spiritual grounding, and the biblically centered evangelicals celebrated their renewed commitment to social ministries. The result has been an avalanche of excellent resources, some in print and others available on-line (sometimes both). I have included some of the most current and best materials that have come to my attention, with an emphasis more on application than analysis (see box at right). I have suggested some examples of the best current materials that have addressed particular issues and expanded the options in the practice of ministry.

You can choke to death on too much material as easily as starve to death on too little. I wrote this book because I found ample information by specialists and consultants, and too little material drawn from the actual experiences of churches in developing social ministries. Specialists can give directions and focus issues, but often

---

INTRO. 1
COMMUNITY RESOURCES: OVERVIEW

Dennison, Jack. *City Reaching: On the Road to Community Transformation.* Pasadena, Calif.: Willilam Carey Library, 1999.

Harper, Nile. *Urban Churches: Vital Signs.* Grand Rapids: Eerdmans, 1999.

Perkins, John. *Restoring At-Risk Communities.* Grand Rapids: Baker Books, 1995.

a few choice words from other leaders in the trenches can resolve issues and inspire action in uniquely powerful ways.

Reviewing the collected sources of this book, I recognize that there is too much to digest at any one time. This is not a single epic to be told in one sitting, but a selection of stories that need to be added to the conversation when necessary. I hope that the wide variety and earthy particularity will provide resources for congregational leaders to deal with the problems that are bound to occur in mobilizing community ministries. I would hope you hear the voices of these ministries as friends and prayer-partners, whom I have shared through the pages of this book as "we" who are together in our commitment to social ministry—researchers and pastors, lay leaders, volunteers, and participants of all sorts. "We" are unseen but available as encouragement that you too can reach out to make a difference through your community ministry.

PART I
Social Context

Social Context

People launch community ministries because they care—not just rationally, but with an irresistible sense of compassion. When members become concerned about community neighbors, when we recognize that problems must be faced, then community analysis can be helpful. In the strong, sustaining love of God, discovering that you care about your community is the first and basic foundation of social ministry. Community analysis is simply a process of naming and ordering information so that you can do something about it.

Our faith also requires a solid foundation for social ministry with a tough-minded community analysis. To share with others in building ministry, we must see the world as clearly as possible. Without such a hard-eyed re-examination, our familiarity and our prejudices will bind us to the past and blind us to problems, trends, and new possibilities. A community study should:

- shift our concern from ourselves to others around us;
- support and/or challenge what we expected to find;
- help us see changes and trends in our community;
- bring out into the open the hopes and fears that have only been whispered privately;
- provide a basis for focusing our social ministries;
- locate resources and allies that share our commitments;
- set our particular concerns in a regional and world context; and
- provide contacts and materials to help us interpret our ministry to a wider audience.

In community analysis we use a progression of steps that move from gathering more objective information, to reflecting on and probing the information, to the point of a committee's making preliminary decisions on the focus of ministry. In the initial data gathering, I offer two steps that focus first on places and then on people. Some action groups or local committees may want to begin with a focus on people (step two), but I suggest that you first define the boundaries of your community and then describe the people who inhabit it.

STEP 1. DEFINE YOUR COMMUNITY

You can define your community from many approaches, but we will focus on three: (a) chart the physical boundaries, (b) identify the anchor institutions, and (c) look for the gathering places.

STEP 2. IDENTIFY THE PEOPLE

I suggest three perspectives: (a) observe populations and lifestyles, (b) note historical changes and current trends, and (c) review statistical summaries.

Once you gather the basic information that defines the community and describes the people, your committee should move to a second level of reflecting on the material and probing its implications. For many groups, the interesting—perhaps explosive—material comes through in their follow-up explorations. Steps 3, 4, and 5 are related: As you recognize invisible people, you can begin to trace the intangible forces, and your sensitivity to both will be expanded by the people you interview.

STEP 3. FIND THE "INVISIBLE" PEOPLE

Every community has people who are ignored, marginalized, or simply out of sight. By identifying these groups, your committee and the congregation become more sensitive to a range of conditions in your community.

Step 4. Analyze the Intangible Forces.

Just as churches have always been concerned with spiritual forces, you should identify the social, economic, political, and religious forces operating in your community. These forces may be intangible, but they are real incentives and barriers in the lives of the people you are trying to reach and in the development of your ministry.

Step 5. Listen to Your Community

Using this wealth of data and feelings, you can initiate conversations with a wide variety of people from every segment of community life.

The final level of analysis invites you to draw together the themes of your study and insights of your conversations to make a tentative choice for a social ministry. Note that the same issues that you uncover in community study are relevant as your church seeks to reach out in a variety of ministries, from pastoral care to evangelism, from vacation Bible school to stewardship of community resources. As you explore a variety of possible ministries, you may shift the focus of your study, but basic questions remain: What are your natural, functional communities, and who are your marginalized peoples? What are the most evident human needs, and how effective is your community response? What does the Gospel call you to do, and who might be allies in this ministry?

Step 6. Choose Your Focus of Ministry

Although a firm decision on the appropriate ministry depends on finding a comfortable fit between your social context and your congregational identity, I encourage you to bring your community analysis into focus by deciding on a possible ministry (or ministries). This preliminary inclination toward a particular ministry will be helpful in later discussions.

Define Your Community

The first task in gathering information is to define your community. Often this step challenges our Christian conscience, reminding us that all people of the community are—or should be—the focus of our Christian concern.

How then will you define your community? To combine the objectivity of study with the compassion of faith, we use three complementary approaches: (a) chart the physical boundaries, (b) identify the anchor institutions, and (c) look for gathering places. These approaches move us from the objectivity of an observer, through the framework of institutions, to the intimacy of belonging that holds the community together. You may gather extensive data, but you can summarize the information in two or three pages, along with the maps and documents that bring it to life.

CHART THE PHYSICAL BOUNDARIES

Boundaries are the easiest and most obvious starting point for identifying your community. Physical boundaries include major streets, highways, and railroad tracks, or natural barriers such as hills, valleys, and rivers. When your committee agrees on your community boundaries, you will have a basis for visualizing the community together throughout your study.

For most churches, at one time the members lived in the community and knew the neighborhood. But American economic and social mobility has confused such simplicity, and now many members no longer live in the old community. Therefore, most churches, both Protestant and Catholic, need to identify both the immediate area in which they provide primary service to people in need and a larger region where their members live.

The terms sometimes become confusing, since some Protestants call the smaller service area a "parish," while Catholics are more likely to use "parish" for a larger area of membership residence. For very practical reasons in developing social ministries, we use parish to refer both to the members who live in the neighborhood and to their concern for ministry to everyone in their community.

Even as you define your community to help you choose your ministry, so also your selection of ministry may help you define your community. As these examples from churches suggest, ministry and community are closely related.

Calumet Park Covenant Church

A suburban church bordering a major city defines its parish boundaries in this way. Notice how members' sense of mission helps to define their service community:

> The boundaries of our church project service area is Calumet Park, with portions of the city overlapping to the north and east starting north to 119th, south to 131st, east to Halsted, and west to Winchester. We wanted to include the portions of Chicago to the north and east because:
>
> 1. They are our neighbors.
> 2. We have members in those surrounding areas.
> 3. It is a part of our outreach ministry program.

Washington Street Presbyterian Church

Sometimes physical barriers define the parish, as in the case of this congregation that tries to make the most of highly recognized boundaries.

> The physical boundaries of railroad tracks and switching yards, heavy industry, the White River, and Central State Mental Hospital isolate the neighborhood from surrounding areas of the city as well as divide it internally. This isolation and internal division (exacerbated today by racial boundaries) had made political and community organizing difficult. It has only been in the last few years that basic city services like repair of streets and sidewalks, Crime Watch, and Community Development Block Grant programs have been available to us.

Leet Memorial and Boyd's Grove United Methodist Churches
Concerned Christians in a rural community define their community and
service area in a combination of geography, geology, and history that reflects
their orientation to their land. Notice how they still conclude with defining
their service area by their concern for ministry:

> Our community is . . . situated in the northeast corner of Stark
> County in Osceola Township. The town rests on a large fertile
> plateau geologically known as the Camp Grove Ridge since the
> ridge was formed by a glacial deposit. The service area of our
> project would take in a ten-mile radius around and including our
> town. Within this area are what might easily be termed pockets of
> poverty. These are small burgs that once were incorporated villages
> that due to population losses are no longer viable communities
> providing even the minimum of services.

Ridge Lutheran Church
Some kinds of ministry must be located not by geography but rather by the
participation of a particular population that transcends location. In this
example from the leadership of the Deaf Community, the absence of physical
boundaries becomes part of their identity:

> Because their communications access to the hearing world is
> limited, deaf and hearing impaired persons tend to socialize together
> and . . . most deaf adults marry other deaf adults. This pattern of
> socialization and intermarrying identifies the reality of a Deaf
> Culture in many cities across the country. Deaf people have . . . a
> sense of community.

Clarity about location strengthens most community ministries. When
you have agreed on your boundaries, you may want to make a simple
map of the area. But physical characteristics alone do not define a
community. In many places major institutions are more influential in shaping
people's lives.

IDENTIFY THE ANCHOR INSTITUTIONS

In many communities, significant institutions shape a way of life. These anchor institutions are often ignored by the citizens, who seem to accept them as "the way things are around here." But institutions like schools, hospitals, prisons, military bases, and recreational facilities can define the community in the same way that rivers and mountains define the land.

Such institutions are more than sources of employment—they shape the mood, the needs, the rhythm, and the attitudes of a community. They make a difference even for people who are not directly dependent upon them. They are especially significant for people who want to challenge or change the political or economic establishment.

Anchor institutions provide basic sources of power and decision making in the community. By "anchor institution" we imply our ambivalence. Like a ship's anchor, they provide stability in a storm. But they may also prevent us from moving forward in calm or changing times. In your social analysis, identify these major institutions and explore their implications for your ministry.

Manchester Church of the Brethren

This church, located in an agrarian town, easily identifies several anchor institutions that hold the community in place and provide its basic livelihood:

> The major institutions in this community are education, farming, industry, and retirement. In addition to six public schools, there is a small church-related college with 1,000 students and one private grammar school. . . . Farming is also a large institution in the area. Like most farmers, agriculturalists are suffering economic hardship here, and the small family farm is giving way to agribusiness.
>
> Industry has experienced a decline over the last 15 years, but still provides a substantial number of jobs and revenue. We have an oil refinery, a book bindery, a foundry, a playground equipment manufacturer, a plastics producer, a grain elevator, a veal feed distributor, and several smaller plants. Retirement is one of our largest institutions. In a town of 6,000 people, there are two large retirement homes with church affiliation. A Presbyterian home houses 300 residents and the Church of the Brethren home hosts 175 retirees. Together the homes employ more than 200 workers in the health, domestic, and food service industries.

The college is the largest employer and the largest contributor to the economic base of the community. . . . The presence of a college in a small town makes for greater diversity in life here, but also creates an uncomfortable disparity between those with a postsecondary education and those without.

Some churches recognize a single or dominant pivot for economic, social, and often political stability in their community. In the following examples from churches, both reflect a natural ambivalence about the dominant community institutions. The first recognized its economic dependency, and the second saw how much the institution affected their social life as well.

St. Luke's United Methodist Church
Kokomo can be simply described as a predominantly blue-collar, union-oriented city. . . . Delco Electronics and the Chrysler transmission plant . . . account for approximately 40 percent of the jobs, and the other local industries are dependent upon these two simply because a major portion of their business is as suppliers. As Delco and Chrysler go, so goes our economy.

Baptist Temple
Many members of the congregation have connections to the State Hospital through direct employment themselves or of a family member. Local businesses and professionals profit from sales and referrals. In addition . . . some former patients have decided to relocate in town. . . . They often lack skills for independent living, nor are they able adequately to speak and demand services for themselves. Due to their poverty, they become part of the poor, disenfranchised townspeople . . . and many ex-patients live within the church neighborhood.

Unfortunately these institutions are most evident when they make changes that threaten the community. Such changes often provide the basis for developing ministry. This report laid the groundwork for a ministry with broken families and battered women:

South Chicago Covenant Church
Economically, the loss of the steel industry has changed the stable character of the area; as jobs go, so do the people. . . . Further, there are taverns on every third corner in the residential streets surrounding the church. The rate of alcoholism is high. Family unity is threatened by the sudden "poverty" brought on by the mills closing. This area, once proud and prosperous, has lost its sense of identity and direction.

LOOK FOR GATHERING PLACES

One of the most helpful recent innovations in community study is the affirmation of relationships and associations as assets even in communities of economic deprivation. Every neighborhood has places where people gather for economic, social, political, and religious activities. Churches are obvious gathering places, as are parks, schools, service clubs, taverns, and street corners. Not only restaurants but other local businesses can also be gathering places, well-worn spots where neighbors exchange greetings and gossip along with goods and services. Your community analysis should include a survey of the businesses and agencies that serve the community and the churches and voluntary groups that reflect the values of the residents.

> **I.1**
> **RESOURCES FOR**
> **ASSESSING COMMUNITY ASSETS**
>
> Kretzmann, John. *A Guide to Capacity Inventories: Mobilizing the Community Skills of Local Residents.* Evanston, Ill.: Asset-Based Community Development INstitute, 1997.
>
> Kretzmann, John, and John L. McKnight. *Building Communities from the Inside Out: A Path toward Finding and Mobilizing a Community's Assets.* Evanston, Ill.: Center for Urban Affairs and Policy Research/Northwestern University, 1992.
>
> For additional information:
> *www.nwu.edu/IPR/abcd.html*

In surveying the community gathering places, you will find an affinity with some particular groups and locations. You may be attracted to the gathering places where you are personally comfortable or to locations where other distinct groups are known to gather. As you affirm the assets of these places, you may begin to identify community problems that may be the first clear indication of the issues that your ministry will eventually address.

Most churches list other churches in their surveys of gathering places. Generally, committee members gravitate toward those churches that depend upon similar theological or social strata of community life, not because they have worked together, but more often because they have competed with these churches for prospective members. Yet in this new ministry other congregations may become allies and partners. Cooperation in social ministries can be deeply satisfying; it can provide a common ground for transcending differences, easing tensions, and sharing the movement of the Spirit in our midst.

The following three examples seem to catch the unique beat—and perhaps even the melody—of community life in each location. The first is from a small river town in middle America where the proud past lives on, but the social fabric of the rural economy is struggling for survival. Notice the historic and political tint to these gathering places:

> *Immaculate Conception Catholic Church*
> In the county are 33 churches . . . [and] five school systems (K-12). Other features of the county include the Marshall-Putnam Farm Bureau, Marshall County Historical Society, three nursing homes, four major grain elevators, the light company, committees for both political parties, 4-H groups, and the County Extension Office. Marshall County has the oldest annual celebration in the state, Old Settlers Day, which was first held in 1870. The most significant socioeconomic feature of the community has been agriculture.

You might have guessed that this social ministry generated support for a large community building that is now used by all age groups, especially the elderly. Comparing that rural survey to the view of an urban group, we see increased specialization and a growing tension in franchise operations that threaten local merchants. The committee members begin with businesses they know, then move on to social clubs and neighborhood activities, and finally note what they consider the active churches. Later these layers of neighborhood networks provide the strategy for the congregation's approach to community support for their social ministry:

West Park Christian Church
Businesses in the service area include a major bank branch, a credit union, two owner-operated funeral homes, an independent insurance agency, a CPA, one doctor's office, one lawyer's office, two small owner-operated grocery stores, two printing companies, one owner-operated bakery, two fast-food chain restaurants, two locally operated restaurants, one tavern/restaurant, one owner-operated barber shop, several beauty shops (some operating out of homes), and one convenient dairy/ice cream franchise. An AFL/CIO union hall, a fire station, a city park, and several service fraternities, including a VFW, Masonic Lodge, and Rebekah and Oddfellows Lodge, are located in the . . . service area. The active churches in the area include [ours], St. Anthony's Catholic, Washington Street Methodist, St. Luke's Chapel, Missionary Baptist, and Hawthorn Baptist Chapel.

The third survey picture is equally urban, but it reflects a mixture of middle-class and marginal households in an African American community. What begins as a simple list of businesses becomes a vivid picture of community activity that challenges people to support their outreach ministry:

Riverside Park United Methodist Church
Small businesses in the area are: five beauty shops, two barber shops, a grocery store, cleaners, TV repair shop, fish market, service station, neighborhood tavern, restaurant, three or four pea-shake gambling joints, a 500 liquor store. . . . The community's changing trends include deteriorating and boarded buildings, traffic blockage by double-parked automobiles, commercial trucks at a local business, and people on streets in "vice areas."

FINDING KEY EXAMPLES

When you have completed step 1, you should have a brief report that summarizes your findings and defines your community through (a) the physical boundaries, (b) the anchor institutions, and (c) the gathering places. You may have gathered many pages of materials, but a summary of a few pages helps your committee to focus and provides materials that can be shared with others. You may also have gathered and constructed maps and other supporting documents that give visual impact to your brief report.

The strength of your report lies in finding those few key symbolic phrases and examples which capture community needs and resources in ways that are significant to the members of the congregation.

Identify the People

Relationships are at the center of the Christian faith—that is, relationships with our Lord and within the church family. Many planning committees in the communities that we studied related more easily to people than to physical definitions of the community. We began with boundaries, institutions, and gathering places so that we could focus more clearly on particular people. Your committee might get into this section by telling stories of your experiences in living, working, struggling, suffering, and celebrating with the people around you.

Although stories of individuals may be the best way to get inside the lives of people, in order to shape a ministry we must associate individuals with larger groups based on characteristics they share. But how can we categorize them? We want to avoid stereotyping people and losing touch with the uniqueness of each person, yet some characteristics provide important categories that they themselves would claim:

- distinctive racial, ethnic, or cultural history;
- religious beliefs and affiliations with religious groups;
- education, employment, and income (class) differences;
- age, gender, and sexual orientation;
- family size, age, and life-cycle situation; and
- community location, size, and economic orientation.

Three ways that you might gather information about the people of your community: (a) observe populations and lifestyles, (b) note historical changes and current trends, and (c) review statistical summaries.

OBSERVE POPULATIONS AND LIFESTYLES

Describe the community by the people who inhabit it. Sometimes this can be an explosive exercise since the more familiar you are with the area, the less likely you are to agree about the populations you recognize and their common characteristics. Agreeing on this complex tapestry of similarities, differences, events, and experiences can be energizing and also exhausting.

> **I.2**
> **Resources for Community Analysis**
>
> Percept in Costa Mesa, Calif.: *www.perceptnet.com/*
>
> Visions-Decisions in Atlanta, Ga.: *www.visions-decisions.com/*
>
> For background on clustering populations:
> Weiss, Michael. *Clustering of America.* New York/San Francisco: Harper & Row, 1988; Perennial Library, 1989.

Remarkable new materials have become available with the advanced technologies of the past few years. Denominational offices, universities, and city planning departments are excellent resources for information about local populations, and some independent agencies offer information services with action plans for religious groups. But statistical information does not have the same power as a graphic presentation, like a map by which people can see themselves and others. In graphic form it can more easily be absorbed into the congregational consciousness.

In transcribing information, you may discover strong and sometimes controversial feelings about well-known citizens and particular segments of the community. Congregations (like other human communities) rarely remember events in the same way, and our interpretations reveal as much about us as we are saying about the people and events we describe. Take time to explore your own feelings even as you are describing others who share your neighborhood. In this discussion your committee members come to understand each other better and to recognize the differences each one brings to the decisions for ministry.

Community analysis requires your committee to measure your own memories and experiences by talking with a variety of people in the area. The "windshield survey" is one popular method of summarizing your observations of the habits and lifestyles of community people. In addition to driving, your committee should spend time walking through selected areas, talking with people, and making notes on your observations and experiences.

what is a windshield survey?

The only real experts on the community are the people who live and work there. Let your windshield survey be a way to summarize your best wisdom on the people and groups that might be seen by a sensitive, informed observer. You might also ask yourselves how you would describe your community to an outsider: What are the broadly human characteristics, and what's unique to your community?

These examples show four ways of "seeing the people" of the community. The first is a middle-class African American neighborhood in a major city, where the committee defines its neighbors by their similarity to the congregation, and defines the congregation by its similarity to people in the neighborhood. Hard work, family values, and community safety provide the bridge between the church and community and foundations for their ministries.

Martin Temple AME Zion Church

Our Church Community is a homogeneous group of stable family households. There is significant communication and cooperation among neighborhood residents. Property values are stable, and the crime rates are relatively low in our tract areas. [Our church] shares many common values and characteristics with the surrounding community and therefore flourishes. [Our membership] is composed of hard-working black homeowners and household renters. More than 50 percent are lifelong residents.

From another part of the same large city comes a typical windshield survey that describes the people in two quite different corridors:

Immanuel Lutheran Church

Edgewater and Uptown are two of the most racially diverse [areas] in the city. As an example, Hayt Elementary has students with 16 different native languages. . . . High-rise apartment buildings line the lakefront and house more affluent residents. Paralleling Sheridan just one and two blocks to the west are Winthrop and Kenmore Streets, referred to in the community as the Winthrop-Kenmore Corridor . . . the housing area for the low- or no-income families. Renovation has been going on there for the last few years but the Corridor still houses many low-income residents of different racial and ethnic backgrounds.

The next windshield survey challenges any stereotypes we might harbor as we drive through the bucolic beauty of rural America. What were once homogeneous farming communities now feel divided socially, abandoned economically, and fractured politically. This description laid the groundwork for a ministry to recover and reknit a sense of community:

> *Deer Creek Presbyterian Church*
> Two distinct socioeconomic groups of people live in the area. The largest property-owning group, the permanent family farmer, lives in well-kept rural dwellings. They pay the major part of the taxes and create seven of the 13 farm-related businesses located within the project area. The church congregations are made up largely from this group. . . . The second group tends to be a bedroom-community group. They work and spend money outside the area and return to sleep. They live in dwellings of various states of repair and sizes and tend to be short-term residents. The community has no center of industry, business, or shopping. . . . Communication such as telephone is supplied by four exchanges that require long-distance assistance. Two county government and several social agencies serve the community, but are based outside the four townships. Few social organizations cross county lines.

Finally, a civic-minded congregation in a larger community uses housing as an index of lifestyle and economic class. This description embraces even greater diversity, reflecting an inclination to think of larger community-wide issues for ministry (see fig. 3):

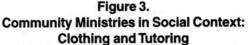

Figure 3.
Community Ministries in Social Context:
Clothing and Tutoring

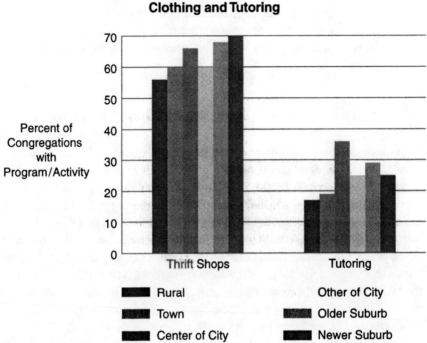

St. Luke's United Methodist Church

Geographically, Kokomo can be easily divided into socioeconomic re-gions. . . . The upper-middle class can be found in the southwestern and northeastern corners of the city. The majority of these people are two-income families of professional and semiprofessional workers. They live in conventionally built homes and have children. The middle class can be found in the west central and south central part of the city. Many of these families have two incomes and are blue-collar workers. They live in prefabricated homes and seem to spend most of their discretionary income on vehicles and recreation.

Although the black community lives predominantly in the east central part of the city, blacks can be found in many other areas of Kokomo also. There is no true ghetto in Kokomo. The blacks live in 35-year-old bungalows and two-story homes—some converted into multiple-family dwellings. . . . The lower economic class of whites can be found in the southeastern part of the city. The entire area is run down with the prefabricated homes in poor repair. There is low-income government housing and a considerable amount of junk strewn about. This area seems more depressed than the black area.

NOTE HISTORICAL CHANGES AND CURRENT TRENDS

Your understanding of community will be incomplete if you focus only on the present situation. A sense of history gives depth and meaning to current conditions. Just as you began your study of populations with a sharing of personal experiences, so you may be stimulated by sharing your own memories of change and your awareness of trends. Where possible, you might form a subcommittee on history with these same two tasks: one, to explore the roots of the present in the extended events of the past and, two, to find the current trends that suggest the shape of the future. History gives unique insight into the causes for oppressive conditions; current trends help identify the unfolding issues. Both are essential in the focus for your social ministry.

Strangely, your committee is most apt to bog down in the historical study, partly because it is endless, but more because it is controversial. A few committees become hypnotized by the information, but more become gun-shy about conflicting viewpoints. Approached with courage and fairness, your studies of history and trends can stimulate congregational interest and help focus your ministry where the need may be greater and the impact may correspond with tides that shape the future of your community.

This white Protestant church uses a simple historical memory to remind one about current social and political realities of their community. With this reminder, the church began a new cooperative ministry with a neighborhood Catholic church.

Avondale Presbyterian Church

[Our community] was originally a separate town in the farmlands to the northwest of Chicago. It was settled by European immigrants who established a town along the railway line. . . . In particular, three groups settled here: Poles, Germans, and Irish, most of them Roman Catholic. [We] remain a neighborhood with strong ethnic identities.

An African American congregation remembers with bitter frustration their efforts to move into a previously all-white community, but derives energy for today from the crisis of the past.

Calumet Park Covenant Church

As blacks continued to move in, it set off an array of real estate activity. . . . Some Realtors tried to have a sellathon by telling the whites this was the last chance for top dollars, playing on their fears. Others blocked advertising of houses for sale. Bankers/ mortgagers began redlining the area, refusing home loans and improvements, etc. In spite of all this, we survived, and we are now an integrated community, thanks to the help of some of the citizens.

When significant changes break into congregational consciousness, they often point to issues that can be translated into ministries. In this small town, the committee recognized a shift in employment patterns as a basis for ministry with children:

Fisher United Methodist Church

Through the years, there has been a shift from heavy dependence on agriculture toward being a bedroom community whose residents work largely outside the community. This has resulted in a large number of children of grade-school age who have both parents working outside the community and not returning until about six P.M. Visible results of this can be seen in the number of children roaming the streets after school [and] . . . an [increased] vandalism in the community.

Many churches point to positive changes in the community to build optimism and support for their ministry. This city church sees a relationship between a population shift and new sidewalks, both signs of hope:

Washington Street Presbyterian Church

The purchasing of older homes by younger couples and families and the fixing-up of those homes is evidence of the upswing of the area. . . . New sidewalks and curbs are evidence of the city's interest in the area. A more active young adult population (ages 25-40) is becoming evident in the neighborhood and community center programs and services, suggesting the emergence of a more vital neighborhood population with the education and resources to create growth and change.

REVIEW STATISTICAL SUMMARIES

Statistical materials have a reassuring, firm objectivity, especially in comparison with our personal experiences and impressions. By reducing attributes to numbers we can make comparisons among populations and across time. We can introduce more kinds of information into the discussion. Your community study will be suspect if you fail to support your concerns with statistics or, on the other hand, if statistics are all you offer. Both narrative and statistical materials are essential.

Statistics are understandably offensive to some people, especially in the church. Statistics reduce people to digits and replace names with numbers. We know, for example, that some basic issues cannot be reduced to numbers, and some people are overlooked or ignored or have good reasons to refuse to be counted. Often subjective judgments enter into the choice of questions, the methods of study, the selection of data, and the style of presentation. There are good reasons to worry about statistical reports.

Even with these limitations, statistical reports are important. They broaden our base of information and include segments of the population that might otherwise be ignored. Broadly based statistical information will inform the committee, support the proposal to sponsoring groups, and help you to interpret your ministry in the church and the community.

The primary source for statistical information is the U.S. Census, even though its accuracy has been seriously challenged. Other sources include libraries, schools, planning boards, utilities, and chambers of commerce; in addition, a variety of government, business, professional, social, and religious agencies collect specialized data. You do not need much, but it must be on target for the questions you are asking.

To see the impact statistics can have, compare these two reports. Both represent farming communities with the same concerns, but the first report only discusses the issue, while the second supports its claim with the facts:

West Street Christian Church
Being a rural community might lead one to assume that agriculture
... has the greatest impact on the majority of residents. However,
statistics indicate that lack of job availability on many levels is
more likely to head the list of concerns.

St. Mary's Catholic Church, Alexandria (projected figures)
The projected population shows a decline in the population for
almost all our towns ... ranging from -.09 to -16.5%. The decline
is due to the closing of several of the General Motor plants in our
area . . . and also the decreasing number of farmers:

	1950	1970	1990	2010
(est)				
# of farms	2,297	1,621	1,346	1,126
# of acres farmed	241,106	235,405	229,677	222,300

By contrast, this city parish uses statistics in two ways—first to develop
a profile of community problems and then to compare its community with
others. Even if we resist the first more formal approach, we are moved by
the second:

Good News Community Church
[Our community] is 14 square blocks with the following
demographics according to the most recent census:

- Total population 6,309 in 2,586 households for an average
  household size of 2.4.
- White 37 percent, Black 31 percent, Hispanic 27 percent, Other
  5 percent.
- 2,420 of the households are renter occupied, and 1,151 are
  without vehicles.
- Average household income is $23,622 with a per capita income
  of $8,550 and a median income of $18,879.
- 61.3 percent of the households earn less than $20,000 per year.
- 30 percent of the population is under the age of 19; 47 percent
  is under the age of 24.

The Children's Defense Fund reports that children such as those who live in [our neighborhood] are "twice as likely to die in the first year of life, to see a parent die, to be suspended from school, and to be unemployed as teens. They are three times as likely to be murdered between the ages of five and nine, to be in foster care, and to die of known child abuse. They are four times as likely to be incarcerated between the ages of 15 and 19."

Statistics can also help us define nongeographic communities by their problems and common concerns:

Ridge Lutheran Church
The unemployment rate among the (deaf) population was four times greater than that of hearing adults, and the level of employment was primarily fixed at unskilled or semi-skilled positions. . . . Clearly one factor affecting the kinds of jobs deaf adults were finding was their limited educational opportunities.

SUMMARIZE YOUR LEARNINGS

When you have finished step 2, summarize your learnings in one or two pages, and add any informative materials you have gathered, such as (a) populations and lifestyles, (b) historical changes and current trends, and (c) supporting statistical summaries.

NEXT STEPS: EXPLORING BELOW THE SURFACE

Steps 1 and 2, defining the place and describing the people, are foundational for community analysis. They provide a solid basis to address the needs and issues of people you minister with. This descriptive and statistical information will help your committee decide about a ministry and interpret that program to potential supporters.

Many community studies stop at this point. People and places are significant, but most church groups need more time to probe the implications of their findings and explore the dynamics of community change. Steps 3, 4, and 5 ask you to look below the surface in three ways: find the invisible people, analyze the intangible forces, and listen to the community. These three areas of study feed each other, and they work best when done simultaneously.

Your follow-up explorations will lead you to probe not only the life of your community, but also your own faith commitments. The question of invisible people encourages you to search for those who are most marginalized and in need of assistance. Sometimes that search reveals our own preconceptions or habitual blindness to people in pain or to sources of power.

As you analyze the intangible political, economic, cultural, or religious forces, your committee may uncover a variety of possible ministries. Intangible forces are often the least subject to documentation, the most sensitive in committee discussion, and the most significant in the choice and the development of your ministry.

Listening to the community is part of every step of social analysis. But when combined with your search for invisible people and your exploration of intangible forces, your interviews should be able to recognize more diverse groups of people and ask more focused questions.

Some church groups feel the urgency to begin ministry without further information gathering, discussion, and delay. The search for invisible people and intangible forces is not just an exercise to be completed en route to ministry, but a discipline of social awareness that should be incorporated in the working habits of every sensitive Christian ministry.

Find the "Invisible" People

The search for people who are invisible to you invites a fresh look at familiar turf. It helps you discover marginalized people whom you may have ignored—or seen so frequently that they have blended into the landscape. Further, as we look at the community through the eyes of these invisible people, we see the church in a new and less complimentary light. We find ourselves asking new kinds of questions about ourselves and our Christian commitments. We take a closer look at the motivations and effectiveness of our church's mission and recognize more clearly our limitations.

L3

RESOURCES FOR SENSITIVITY TO MARGINALIZED PEOPLES

Carlson-Thies, S., et al., eds. *Welfare in America: Christian Perspective in Crisis*. Grand Rapids: Eerdmans, 1996.

Golden, Renny. *Disposable Children: America's Welfare System*. Belmont, Calif.: Wadsworth Publishing Co., 1997.

Many churches celebrate these new discoveries and welcome the opportunity to respond. They use their new discoveries to generate energy in support of the ministries they choose. They see the need to help in ways that empower the alienated people and do not perpetuate the conditions they seek to change.

In fact, we limit social ministry when we begin by asking only, "What are the needs of people in our community?" This can be a condescending approach taken by people in positions of social, political, and economic power. We might better begin with the perspective of the marginalized, powerless, invisible people and ask, "What needs to be changed to make this a just society?" Or to put the question in a more prophetic form, "How can this society be helped to conform to the will of God?"

IN THE MARGINS OF OUR MINDS

In refocusing on these marginal people, we may discover forms of alienation, injustice, and oppression perpetuated by our community neighbors and even church members. We begin to see failures in institutions we have trusted and people we know well. The sin in our systems and in ourselves confronts us.

Students of the Bible have long recognized the special attention God devotes to "widows and orphans," the biblical symbol of invisible people in every society. Many churches have been energized to launch a social ministry when they discovered the marginal lives of neighbors, especially the poor and elderly:

> *Irvington United Methodist Church*
> The invisible folk are the elderly. . . . In many of the apartments older persons are present, but unseen. Many of the homes are owned by aged persons, some of whom have neither the strength [nor] financial resources to maintain property. Some are in churches and participate in community groups; others seem to withdraw behind drapes and doors to watch TV.

> *Lafayette Church of the Brethren*
> [Our community] has been either fortunate or unfortunate, depending on one's biases, in the area of low visibility of its poor. Many times hidden and off the main paths in the city, they are consigned to pockets within the city, as in the near south end. Their presence contradicts the comfort index of a great majority of the area's population and calls for better and more deliberate response from the city's institutions, public and private alike.

Churches also frequently mention physically and mentally handicapped people who have been deinstitutionalized:

> *Baptist Temple*
> [Other] invisible persons could be mental patients discharged from Central State, who settle in the area with no established support network to help them establish stability, find employment, and become "visible" in the community.

Not all the invisible people are poor or handicapped. Many are long-time residents and even respected citizens who have been pushed by economic forces beyond their control. Consider this narrative from a community large enough to have many of the conditions of an urban area, yet small enough for people to know each other's personal problems:

Community United Church of Christ

Some of the invisible people are the unemployed and those affected by area layoffs, as well as those urged by their companies into an unanticipated early retirement. The new homeless forced out of homes by inability to pay mortgages can be hidden in the households of relatives. Teenagers barred from their parents' homes and moving from one friend's house to another could also be termed invisible. Single parents struggling with bills and survival issues fall in that category. The elderly for whom aging means increasing isolation become invisible to us too. There is no specific area that is considered or identified as a pocket of poverty, but invisible people are scattered throughout the community in their own private pockets of poverty and deprivation, unable to recognize their own powers to improve their situations. The isolation factor contributes to the lack of empowerment.

Not everyone finds or wants to find these hidden problems. Some committees doubt the existence of invisible people who need to be incorporated into the larger community:

Deer Creek Presbyterian Church

It is hard to identify any invisible people. It appears that there are none. When contacting the local electric utility, they did not indicate that there was any visible problem to them.

More frequently, however, the discovery of invisible people mobilizes a church to help them personally and to challenge the institutions that have contributed to their conditions:

Washburn Christian Church

The invisible people . . . feel powerless. In the senior citizens apartments . . . they feel insecure as the apartments' emergency cords only turn on the light in the hallway . . . Our committee found out these apartments were not subsidized and were supposed to be. We wrote a few letters to the Federal Housing Authority and circulated a petition among our churches. Within a few weeks the rent was cut by $100 in most cases. They also filled up the units, since it was not so costly.

The challenge of invisible people is not only to recognize them, but also to give them voice so that they can speak for themselves.

Analyze the Intangible Forces

Your committee should plan at least one discussion of the social, economic, political, and religious forces operating in your community. Using the material you have gathered to date, set aside time to explore your options for ministry and the intangible forces that form incentives or barriers to each. Your discussion will probably include:

- laws that affect the groups of people you want to reach;
- mobility, prejudice, and possible limits on outsiders;
- cultural values toward family, education, and leadership;
- employment, changing markets, and future job security;
- "powers and principalities" of the local leader network;
- religious convictions and spiritual powers in our world; and
- personal and group awareness of oppression and affirmation.

L4
RESOURCES TO IDENTIFY
INTANGIBLE FORCES

Livezey, Lowell, ed. *Public Religion and Urban Transformation: Faith in the City.* New York: New University Press, 2000.

Meyers, Eleanor Scott, *Envisioning the New City: A Reader on Urban Ministry.* Louisville: Westminster John Know, 1992.

We can easily identify intangible forces with sources of power in the community, such as dominating employers, entrenched political figures, dysfunctional educational systems, and the like. But we must also recognize the bias in our own perspectives. When our religious commitments come into conflict with our economic, political, and social self-interest—as often happens when we develop or work with a social ministry—our faith is measured more by what we do than what we say.

Intangible forces add a new dimension to the story of ministry, showing the muscle beyond the statistical or narrative descriptions. Frequently congregations with Hispanic or other immigrant people tell of unseen forces that shape their ministries:

Douglas Park Covenant Church

Regardless of statistical changes or trends cited in the data given, there exists a major factor whose impact neither we nor the statisticians will be able to discern for some time to come. With the passing of the new immigration law, the future composition, direction, and progress of our community is uncertain.

A discussion of intangible forces allows church members to wrestle with the differences between the official information and personal experiences. Sometimes the ripple of a trend is felt first by service institutions like the churches and the schools. The official census may say differently, but these people feel the first wave of a change developing:

Washburn Christian Church

Our food distribution lines are quite long these days. Five years ago the churches organized a food pantry. Before that most people had good jobs, so there was simply no need for it. It is obvious that plant layoffs began a vicious cycle of unemployment, hunger, and people moving away looking for something better. As more moved, businesses closed in town and houses began being boarded up. Business closing locally causes more unemployment and more empty houses.

Intangible forces include the values we share that hold us together, that sometimes evolve into ministries (see figure 4).

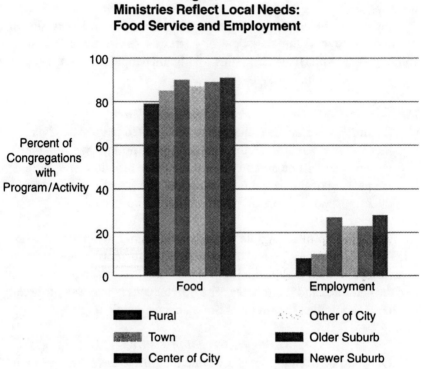

Figure 4.
Ministries Reflect Local Needs:
Food Service and Employment

First Presbyterian Church, Canton
Unemployment is very present . . . and local resources are
declining. . . . Some of our churches receive smaller contributions
and some of our membership are seeking public assistance for
the first time, yet they nevertheless continue to provide these much-
needed social services. Our community is strong and . . . very
supportive of the needs of its people. . . . As our United Way so
aptly puts it, "Canton Is Special."

EMPOWERED BY THE UNSEEN

Intangible forces allow your committee to discuss directly the political and social attitudes that are more elusive in statistical and descriptive reports. This Protestant congregation recognized the weaving of politics and religion in the community and therefore joined with a Catholic group to develop a common ministry:

Hope Presbyterian Church
Springfield has an "old guard," a "good old boy" network, established by lifelong residents of the community. More times than not, to acquire power in this political city you must have been born here. In addition, the power brokers are largely Catholic, not surprising when nearly half of the community is Roman Catholic. . . . There are still the underlying problems of racism, hunger, homelessness, poverty, and unemployment, and the ramifications caused by these "conditions." All the social ills of any metropolitan area are present here, and our church is being called to respond.

Prayer, biblical faith, and courage are essential ingredients for a congregation to strengthen individual voices to look as honestly at themselves as they do at the community they live in. The insights about ambivalence and capitulation in the following observations did not come from a single person but reflect a continuing congregational dialogue about the health of their community:

Lafayette Church of the Brethren
Homeostasis, a "let it be" attitude, [encourages] . . . apathy and unconcern. This overriding sense of stability has impacted our congregation in the same way it has impacted the general religious community. . . . Church people, in response to their faith, are eager to help, to support from their material bounty. [However] . . . there has been a real shying away from advocacy and challenging the structures that undergird the issues that need to be addressed. The problems are bandaged without opening the sore for healing.

Discouragement, even despondency (or worse, apathy), often mark congregations that see no way to respond to the negative forces of their communities. But hope is more characteristic of congregations with social ministries, not because they believe that they are winning, but because they offer members at least an opportunity to express their faith in action.

Immaculate Conception Catholic Church

Economic factors create the primary issues affecting our community. The layoffs in manufacturing, the farm crisis, and the nationwide recession result in many moving away, increased unemployment and underemployment, the need for both parents in a family to work, a decrease in family income, the failure of businesses, economic problems of small towns, and probably increased failures of marriage and a growing alcohol and drug abuse problem. A good result of these discouraging economic factors is a re-evaluation of values. People seem to be becoming more committed to family, church social programs and more responsive to people in need.

STEP 5

Listen to Your Community

With your background of exploring the community, your committee should become more deliberate about your interviews. Your various maps of populations, institutions, and gathering places offer an array of contacts. Your reflections on invisible people and intangible forces should suggest a sharp focus to your inquiry. Your statistical support can add authority and bluntness to your dialogue—you should be able to ask more pointed questions, and to know an appropriate "follow-up" as needed. But, as always, you will gain more when you approach each interview as an informed listener who cares a great deal and who needs to learn what this individual (or group) can teach.

An amazing assortment of people are available and willing to talk with church committees about community ministries. You can reach educators, political figures, community planners, government agency staff, agencies, police officers and judges, business leaders and local shopkeepers, labor officials, reporters, and caregivers in medicine and social services, in programs for the elderly, family, youth, and children. More challenging, you also need to talk with typical citizens who share your concerns (although not necessarily your viewpoint) but are unfettered by institutional connections.

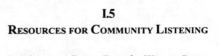

I.5
RESOURCES FOR COMMUNITY LISTENING

Gunderson, Gary. *Deeply Woven Roots: Improving the Quality of Life in Your Community*. Minneapolis: Fortress, 1997.

Medoff, Peter, and Holly Sklar. *The Streets of Hope: The Fall and Rise of an Urban Neighborhood*. Boston: South End Press, 1994.

You will find these interviews helpful in several ways. *First*, you will learn more than the facts of the community. As your committee discovers others who share your concerns and your feelings, you will form relationships with people who see common issues in different ways. You will discover and weave together a network of people who care about many of the same issues and who learn to work together even across your differences.

Second, others will see your church as a concerned neighborhood institution. The people you contact begin to think of the church as a potential partner in the areas of shared concerns. They will treat the church differently and include the church in community meetings it has not been invited to before.

Third, the members of your group begin to see themselves differently. Once they begin the interviews, they realize that they are changing in the process. As others begin to think of the church as a partner and ally, the committee members re-examine the church's ministry and mission. We often find a loop of growing self-confidence: when the church shows interest in the community, others accept the church, and church leaders begin to think and act in more inclusive ways.

You will find that, of all the material you have gathered in your community study, the interviews are the hardest to capture in print. In these interactive experiences, body language and feeling tones have equal impact with spoken words. Therefore, we suggest that your written reports of interviews be simple and brief. List the participants, summarize the conversation, and note any follow-up items and persons responsible.

These first reports are typical of local church interviews with leaders of agencies and institutions. Note the variety of people approached and the way these professionals summarize their concerns in an easy list for the committee to work on. You can see the networks begin to form and loops of self-confidence develop as the churches become more highly esteemed and the community leaders want to be kept informed:

Calumet Park Covenant Church

When one of our members spoke with Dr. J., principal at Calumet School, his response was: "There is a great need for tutoring classes besides the one in the schools, because of the fast transience of youth from the inner-city schools . . ." He wants to be kept informed of our progress. Another member spoke with Mr. McC, a dean and tutor of Dwight D. Eisenhower High School,

[who] agreed that there is a definite need for tutoring and GED classes, for the teenage mothers, dropouts, and students with poor reading and writing skills. . . . He also wants us to keep him abreast of our progress.

Deer Creek Presbyterian Church

Ron W., sheriff, sees (1) alcohol and drug abuse, and (2) vandalism as major problems in the community. Possible help for these problems includes leadership that encourages support of the law-enforcement system, and programs that address the problems and encourage people to get involved. Craig M., agri-business executive, sees our biggest problems as (1) decline of the middle-class farm, (2) relationships between business people and farmers, and (3) drugs. Churches and social agencies need to work together with the help of specialists.

By contrast, interviews with typical residents are usually more rambling and less focused; they are more likely to tell their personal story, and to include more information than you need in a brief interview:

Leet Memorial and Boyd's Grove United Methodist Churches

Fred C., a single parent with three children and receiving public aid, stated that due to his children he feels that something more for children and youth to do would be appropriate. He also stated that the churches contribute a great deal to the community, especially the Methodist Church through its food pantry. He also stated that if a need arose he would feel more comfortable approaching the Methodist Church rather than his own.

St. Mary's Catholic Church, Alexandria

C. H., an interviewee from the food pantry, is 22 years old, legally separated, has two dependents and is expecting a third child. Her immediate need was housing. She is presently renting at $500.00/ mo. plus utilities. She served with the U.S. Army for four and a half years and worked one year as a secretary. She got out of the service last January, and is a lifetime resident of the area. She would like . . . [list of desired ministries].

Some churches use group interviews (discussions) effectively. Such conversations increase participation in a way that both gathers information and develops support for the program. This committee interviewed participants in other church ministries:

Cornell Baptist Church

We conducted one set of interviews with four parents whose children are currently enrolled in our after-school program. Because they have children, their major community concerns were for children and youth. They were also concerned about having activities that would encourage moral values and keep children productive and "out of trouble." . . .

We conducted two interviews with clients of the Community Food Pantry which we house in our building and support as an ecumenical endeavor. They echoed the same concern about education. . . . One woman brought along a copy of the school paper which her daughter edits, but she could only show it to people because she herself cannot read.

You might want to hold a larger group interview like this community meeting that was sponsored by a group of churches to "interview the town" and to generate interest in their project. Even people who could not attend participated by sending letters that were read aloud and incorporated into the summary:

Immaculate Conception Catholic Church

On September 26, a Public Forum was held to gather input and help publicize the existence of the project. It was publicized in the local paper by the committee public relations person, in the churches and by word of mouth. . . . With the combination of discussion and letters submitted by interested persons unable to attend, [these issues emerged]: 1. quality day care, 2. youth center, 3. service for the elderly, 4. latch-key children service, 5. teen volunteer program, and 6. classes to assist and inform the public.

Since interviews create interest, your committee should find ways to share the information you receive and the decisions you reach. Your summaries should affirm all suggestions but push toward a focus for your ministry:

Hope Presbyterian Church

As we began to search for community needs that were both urgent and manageable, we started by polling our own membership. Knowing that we could not address all of the needs discovered, we narrowed our scope to three areas of ministry . . . child-abuse prevention, elderly care, and crisis counseling.

The following report, prepared by a joint committee of two urban churches, contains the basic elements that bring ministry into focus, namely:

- wide variety of representative interviews (in this case an unusually large number of people were contacted);
- general description of the community context for ministry;
- primary areas for ministry and secondary areas of concern;
- resources potentially available for ministry; and
- affirmation of the church's role in social ministry.

First-Meridian Heights Presbyterian Church

An itemization of responses of 49 interviews performed by our joint congregations is available, but here is a summary of these interviews. There were an even number of black and white, male and female, and different age groups represented. Sixteen of the interviews were with residents who had been in the area less than 10 years while 31 were with residents of more than 10 years. We surveyed a wide variety of professions and interest groups. . . . In general, the surveys recognize the neighborhood positively for its general stability at this time, for the diversity of people (age, race, economic mix), for the feelings of pride evident in certain parts of neighborhood, and for the overall quality of housing. The areas of primary concern raised by the majority of the people interviewed were lack of supervised activities and a community resource center for children. This was thought to be related to the development of gangs, loitering, problems with drugs and alcohol. The second most commonly recognized problem in the area was crime, in part thought to be secondary to the lack of adequate supervision after school and on weekends. Further down on the list of priorities were lack of adequate upkeep for properties, poor access to business and other entertainment, and lack of adequate government support in the area. . . . There are a number of resources which are available in the area that were frequently recognized by the interviewees. Perhaps because church members were interviewing, local churches were recognized as the number-one potential resource for improving conditions in the neighborhood.

Interviews rarely simplify the questions; they generally complicate your decision-making with many more options and a much more complex texture of existing conditions and probable causes. But you will come away from these encounters enriched by the discovery of new resources and energized by the need to make a start—somewhere.

DIRECT CONTACT

Steps 3, 4, and 5 combine exploration, reflection, and interviews. This direct contact with institutional leaders and typical citizens will help you gain a richer appreciation for the essential elements of program development and, equally important, a network of relationships with a broad base of people who share your concerns and your commitments to change.

Most committees enjoy this part of the study because they have a chance to express their beliefs and feelings and to explore the underside of communities they have taken for granted. You can summarize in two or three pages what you have learned in steps 3, 4, and 5, with particular focus on the invisible people, the intangible forces, and your interviews with community people.

Choose Your Focus of Ministry

If you have the luxury of time, then your decision for ministry should be informed and solid. Some committees simply do not have time because they begin with a commitment to a particular program, and the community study confirms or shifts their direction. Other committees consider a variety of options, with each new step winnowing down the possibilities and lifting up a few viable alternatives. However you approach it, your committee should now make a preliminary decision. Reports from congregations in the FACT study (fig. 5 on the following page) show the frequency that congregations have chosen particular kinds of ministries.

Figure 5.
Community Outreach Ministries
Listed by Frequency of Response

List of Community Outreach Ministries.............................. YES%

Cash assistance to families or individuals............................ 88%
Food pantry or soup kitchen... 85%
Clothing closet/thrift shop.. 61%
Crisis hotline or counseling... 46%
Hospital or nursing home.. 45%
Senior citizen programs.. 45%
Prison or jail ministry.. 38%
Emergency or affordable housing.. 38%
Day care, etc. for children... 36%
Substance abuse.. 33%
Tutoring or literacy... 32%
Health programs, clinics.. 32%
Advocate justice issues.. 29%
Voter education.. 26%
Employment program... 21%
Migrant/immigrant.. 14%

Faith Communities Today (FACT) A Report on Religion in the United States Today, 2001

Your task is to agree on a brief statement of focus for your new ministry. This statement must be clear enough for other people to see the possibilities and yet remain as an initial draft to be shaped with the participation of others. Your challenge is to articulate your goal in such a way that it can win the affirmation of a much larger group.

Some program developers will request that you state your goal in a single sentence. Although we affirm the need for simplicity and clarity, single-sentence goal statements usually are so broad that they raise as many questions as they resolve. Rather, bring your ministry into focus with just enough detail to provide a basis for action.

Your goal should be specific to a particular community problem and sufficiently limited that you can accomplish it. It should be appropriate to the present time and within the capacity of the supporting groups. Others should be able to recognize its significance if they are to support its goals.

First, here are a couple of single sentence goal statements. While they are worthy goals, they are too global to be translated into specific programs and find either support or success:

Our mission is education for the illiterate.
To work with young people between the ages of 5 and 18.

Negative statements are another problem. A statement of goals set in the context of less desirable alternatives is awkward because it places the emphasis on what it is not:

There is a complexity of problems in this community as in most inner cities: many functionally illiterate adults, malnutrition, unemployment, scarcity of jobs needing the level of skills of this population, child abuse, drug abuse, lack of day care facilities for children and elders, teenage pregnancy, etc. Within this context are housing needs [which the group chose].

On the other hand, this committee uses negative information effectively to heighten interest and challenge commitment to the ministry they are recommending:

Douglas Park Covenant Church

Our community has undergone great change in the last two decades. It can now be described as predominantly Hispanic, young, and low-income. Existing community institutions attempt to deal with social concerns, but with their limited resources they focus on the most severe problems in a crisis intervention style. Often, they are able to offer only Band-Aid solutions. No existing community organization focuses predominately on parent and child education. The lack of this service has encouraged us to focus our project in this area.

As congregations become informed, some committees use the interest created by their interviews as a platform for recommended ministry. This goal statement invites the support of all those interviewed, first affirming their community and then offering a program based on common goals:

Cornell Baptist Church

In summary, people do not feel that the community is improving, but rather declining, as evidenced by more vacant lots, less housing available for low-income households, few community activities for children and youth, concern for children's safety, poor achievement in school, and few jobs available. Two themes ran through the conversations:

1. People care about the quality of education and the renewal of the community, not just opportunities for themselves.
2. People are interested in finding ways to help children and youth develop into educated and productive members of society.

The following statements are focused and brief. They are specific in goal and content, yet broad enough to stimulate community support:

University Park Christian Church

Our goal is to provide a continuum of care for older adults who are unable to remain alone, by drawing on the full range of our congregational and community resources.

St. Mary's Catholic Church, Alexandria

The group probably most resistant to any social ministries is the group we want to target—parents with battered children. . . . They have difficulty in parenting and lack identification of their needs. And they distrust help.

BECOMING REAL

Every step contributes something in shaping community ministry, and the whole picture is greater than any one person's experience. As the program develops, the participants in ministry become real to one another as people under the same God with many common hopes and aspirations.

When your ministry includes both personal contact and time for reflection, together you can recognize and discuss the intangible forces both within individuals and in society, in their shared concern for both spiritual inadequacy and social injustice that become apparent in community ministries. Why should children of God feel so alienated and denied by intangible forces greater than themselves? What can we do for individual people and for the larger social causes of their personal problems? Concern for these religious and political issues is a natural consequence of sharing

> **I.6**
> **RESOURCES FOR**
> **MODELING COMMUNITY MINISTRIES**
>
> Strobel, Charles F. *Room in the Inn: Ways Your Congregation Cn Help Homeless People.* Nashville: Abingdon, 1992.
>
> Temple, Gray, Jr. *52 Ways to Help Homeless People.* Nashville: Thomas Nelson, 1991.

among caring people. We'll look at these issues more fully in subsequent chapters as we consider the identity of the congregation and the organizational structure of ministry.

For now, it is enough to find a place where ministry can make a difference to real people in the immediate community and to begin building together with new friends and allies.

CHECKLIST FOR PART I:

Social Context

Step 1: Define Your Community (pp. 22-30)

We have agreed on our community boundaries for this study.
Date: _____   *Assigned to:*_____

We have identified the anchor institutions and gathering places.
Date: _____   *Assigned to:* _____

We have summarized the information above in a brief working report.
Date: _____   *Assigned to:* _____

Step 2: Identify the People (pp. 31-41)

We have obtained and examined a demographic profile of the community.
Date: _____   *Assigned to:*_____

We have written a summary description of the populations in our community.
Date: _____   *Assigned to:* _____

Step 3: Find the "Invisible" People (pp. 42-45)

We have described the "invisible" or marginalized people in our community, and made efforts to visit with them.
Date: _____   *Assigned to:* _____

Step 4: Analyze the Intangible Forces (pp. 46-50)

We have discussed and summarized the forces that are incentives or barriers to our ministry and to others in our community.
Date: _____   *Assigned to:* _____

Step 5: Listen to Your Community (pp. 51-56)

We have interviewed _____ (enter number) people in our community and have reviewed a brief written report of each interview.
Date: _____   *Assigned to:* _____

We have summarized the interviews, noted opportunities for ministry, and shared the information with our congregation.
Date: _____   *Assigned to:* _____

Step 6: Choose Your Focus of Ministry (pp. 57-60)

We have listed several possible ministries and chosen one or two as our preliminary focus.
Date: _____   *Assigned to:* _____

Congregational Identity

PART II

Congregational Identity

Your study of the social context (Part I) develops a foundation for your community ministry. With a solid base of information and community contacts, your committee has probably become aware of the most urgent individual needs and the most dysfunctional systems. You have a good sense of where you might begin developing a social ministry and some idea about how much work may be involved.

But there is a second dimension to launching a ministry, beyond the data from community analysis or the depth of available resources. To gain the support of your church, the ministry must touch the nerve of congregational concern and speak the language of congregational compassion.

Church members will filter your reported facts and recommendations through their own values and commitments. Nothing will be convincing that is out of sync with the character of the congregation, and few projects will find support if they are at odds with the "kind of church" the members believe they are.

> **II.1**
> **RESOURCES FOR**
> **UNDERSTANDING CONGREGATIONS**
>
> Ammerman, Nancy T., Jackson W. Carroll, Carl S. Dudley, and William McKinney. *Studying Congregations: A New Handbook*. Nashville: Abingdon, 1998
>
> Frank, Thomas Edward. *The Soul of the Congregation: An Invitation to Congregational Reflection*. Nashville, Abingdon, 2000.
>
> Jung, L. Shannon. *Rural Congregational Studies: A Guide for Shepherds*. Nashville: Abingdon, 1997.

Congregational identity incorporates the beliefs and commitments that hold a congregation together, motivate its members, and make it distinctive from others. You can articulate some of beliefs, but many commitments cannot be put into words. Sometimes they are carried quietly in rhythms of ritual and are interpreted only through stories. The church acts out these values and commitments in the patterns of church life—what the church does and how it does it.

Congregational identity, like personal character, takes its shape from the accumulation of experiences. It gives the group coherence and a basis for making decisions. Embedded in congregational identity are the criteria for what is acceptable and the sources of energy for ministry. The congregation, knowing its identity, sifts through and tests the recommendations for a social ministry, as it does with all other decisions. The decision to begin a social ministry is more than a procedural or political process: It is an important affirmation of the basic commitments we share as a community of Christians.

The next task you face, then, is not articulated, though it always needs to happen in some form. To establish your social ministry, your committee will need to find the aspects of your congregation's identity that support your cause. Elements of faith will confirm that it is right to become involved with these issues, and historical precedents will give stature to the ministry you recommend.

Some committees never listen, but always talk, trying to persuade the congregation with a sales pitch for their idea. I encourage you, rather, to explore the character of your congregation, looking for openings that will more naturally give your proposal a place in the active identity of the congregation. Knowing your congregational identity is both energizing and seductive. Examining history and sharing the stories that give the congregation unity and purpose will energize your committee. But some people become so fascinated by their memories that identity becomes an end in itself, distracting them from developing new ministries. Keep in mind the purpose of your explorations: to strengthen your congregation's commitments to ministries of all sorts, including your response to community needs.

Four elements of congregational identity are especially significant in supporting social ministry. The first three form a triangle of insights: from Scripture, tradition, and experience. Your primary sources for this material will be church leaders and official documents. But it is important also to develop a broader base of understanding about your congregation. Therefore, I encourage you to gather information from the members through a survey. I suggest these four steps in exploring your congregational identity:

STEP 1. IDENTIFY YOUR BIBLICAL FOUNDATIONS

Although Scripture is foundational for all Christians, every church shapes its own tradition of understanding the text. The congregation's biblical faith gives us a window that looks two ways. For the church, Scripture is a way to see the world; for identity, Scripture is a way to see the church.

STEP 2. FIND SOURCES IN YOUR HERITAGE

Every congregation keeps alive selected elements from its broad Christian past and more recent denominational heritage. We trace the roots of heritage in creeds and official statements, programs and actions of the larger church, and the "saints" we share with other Christians across the years.

STEP 3. BUILD ON YOUR CONGREGATIONAL HISTORY

You can often predict what kinds of ministry a congregation will support, including social ministries, by looking at the ways members remember their own historical experiences. We will explore congregational history by listening for the stories of who they are as a church, how they got there, and how they have related to the community.

STEP 4. ANALYZE YOUR STRENGTHS AND LIMITATIONS
THROUGH A SURVEY

You can learn a great deal about the values and commitments of the congregation by asking questions of a broad sample of the members. This separate source of information may both confirm and challenge what you have learned from church leaders during the other steps in your identity study.

STEP 1

Identify Your Biblical Foundations

A theological tradition grounded in a biblical faith is basic to the identity of every congregation. Some churches emphasize the theological tradition carried in teaching and sacraments, while other churches put the emphasis on individual relationships with a living God. In both, the Bible is central to faith traditions, and faith traditions carry their interpretation of the Bible.

Functionally, church members differ in the ways we acquire and apply our biblical foundations. We have learned the Bible in different places—from the liturgy and from Sunday school, from personal study and disciplined classes, from the pulpit and the choir. Further, personal experiences may shape the ways we use it: Some of us are comfortable and some hesitant; some proclaim and some are burned out. The task for your committee is to identify your congregation's biblical tradition: How does it hear the biblical faith, and how is that faith seen to support your social ministry?

> **II.2**
> **RESOURCES FOR
> BIBLICAL/THEOLOGICAL FOUNDATIONS**
>
> Brueggemann, Walter. *Using God's Resources Wisely: Isaiah and Urban Possibility.* Louisville: Westminster John Knox, 1993.
>
> Saunders, Stanley, and Charles L. Campbell. *The Word on the Street: Performing the Scriptures in the Urban Context.* Grand Rapids: Eerdmans, 2000.
>
> Wink, Walter. *The Powers That Be: Theology for a New Millennium.* New York, Doubleday, 1998.

Your group has access to the congregation's biblical faith in three broad areas: your assumptions, your proclamations, and your decision-making process. Your assumptions are most compelling because they show how your biblical faith has been absorbed into the thought and habits of individuals and into the patterns of congregational life. We use Scripture most frequently to maintain the assumptions of faith and weave such rehearsals of faith into our church music and prayers, into the gestures and phrases we take for granted until we have forgotten the source ("God be with you" becomes "goodbye"). But important as the study of lingual and behavioral assumptions may be, it is outside the interests of most groups advocating social ministry.

More likely, you can study the proclamation of the biblical tradition as it comes from the pulpit where the text is preached and from all sorts of classes where the faith is taught, shared, and modeled. You can study sermons for content and intent—for what is said and what is assumed, for the requested response and the reaction it actually receives. You can attend classes to learn in interaction with others who attend, discuss, decide, and act in response to questions of faith. You have endless opportunities within the church to explore what people think and believe.

You may find a few decisive moments that offer you an acid test for your biblical tradition: That is, when your congregation makes a decision, what biblical foundation is actually convincing? You can listen to the biblical appeals and warrants that are advanced in the discussion, note the rationale the members offer, and read how they explain the decisions they have made. For our reflections here, we review several basic themes that churches use to explain their decisions to engage in social ministry.

The way the congregation reads the Bible tells them about the text; it also tells the committee about the church. By listening carefully, your committee will be able to find the themes of biblical faith that are important to your congregations. These themes may not be systematic like a theological text; diverse—even contradictory—views are often carried comfortably in the same congregation.

Most congregations anchor their social ministries in a familiar text—for example (as suggested above) in Luke 4:18-19, where Jesus begins his ministry by reading from Isaiah in the synagogue, or in Matthew 25:31ff., where the Son of Man judges the nations according to those who cared for "the least of these who are members of my family." But congregations use these texts (and others) differently, and those differences guide their ministries and reflect their unique styles. In reviewing their biblical foundations for social ministry, we find several themes running through congregational materials. Your committee may recognize one or more of these themes in your own congregation's biblical tradition, and you may find other interpretations that stimulate their support for social ministry.

- We feel called to respond to God's love by sharing salvation with others, or by our concern for all of God's creation.
- We are responsible and obedient to God's expectations, sometimes to serve those in need and sometimes to challenge and change the evil we find.
- We walk with God's presence in and among us through images of Spirit, Jesus, Body of Christ, and Kingdom of God.

"WE FEEL CALLED BY GOD"

Christians—Protestants and Catholics alike—feel called by God to engage in social ministry; it is more than just a personal or rational decision. In a classic comparison, a Protestant church feels the call from the biblical text, while a Catholic parish feels rooted in its sacramental sense of calling:

> *Community United Church of Christ*
> In the New Testament Christ calls to us in Matthew 7:12: "Do for others what you want them to do for you," and in Matthew 5:14-16 we are called into the wider community.

> *St. Mary's Catholic Church, Indianapolis*
> By our baptism we have been called to be disciples and to go and preach the Good News of Jesus. How better to do this than by actions that prove our love for the brokenhearted, the downtrodden and the rejected (Luke 4: 18-19)!

Some congregations hear God calling them to develop and maintain creation; others explicitly reject humanitarian reasons in order to emphasize God's initiative. Although theologians have suggested that these views conflict, we find that either one can motivate a church for social ministry, and some churches affirm both. Compare these two excerpts:

Avondale Presbyterian Church

In Matthew 25:31-46 we are called to service in the name of Our Lord Jesus Christ. Every Sunday in our bulletin we read, "Enter to Worship—Depart to Serve." We are reminded that worship of God does not only take place in church on Sunday, but that we worship God by serving throughout creation.

Cornell Baptist Church

Our church has never been involved in its community for "humanitarian" reasons . . . [but rather for] our understanding of individual and corporate salvation. . . . For us, salvation is more than being "saved from hell"; it is an experience that transforms all of life's priorities, loyalties, behaviors, and relationships. Therefore, our salvation, rather than allowing us to selfishly enjoy or hoard our experience with Christ, calls us to be involved in our world and to share this salvation with our communion.

In responding to God's call, we can be transformed. In this joint statement, two cooperating churches say that social ministry can lift them from self-centered activities and allow them to use their theological differences constructively:

First Meridian Heights Presbyterian Church

"Do nothing from selfishness or conceit, but in humility count others better than yourselves. Let each of you look not only to his own interests, but also the interests of others" (Phil. 2:3-4). . . . Our members recognize that the desire for personal salvation without social redemption is not only selfish but impossible. . . . We have conservative and progressive members enabling our churches to live in a "dynamic middle" rather than a "dead center."

"We Are Responsible and Obedient to God"

The commanding character of biblical passages is a relief to some church members. It is important to this committee that they have willingly responded to God's expectations of them:

Riverside Park United Methodist Church

Jesus spelled out our responsibility as individuals and as a church in Matthew 25:31-46. It was in these verses that he said: "Come, oh blessed of my Father, inherit the kingdom prepared for you from the foundation of the world; for I was hungry and you gave me food, I was thirsty and you gave me drink, I was a stranger and you welcomed me, I was naked and you clothed me, I was sick and you visited me, I was in prison and you came to me."

Whether by call or by obedience, congregations engaged in prophetic ministries see God as the source of authority. This emphasis on justice has a different priority in various denominational groups, and differs in congregations within these faith traditions (see fig. 6). Congregations do not act on their own, but they respond to God's expectations to change the social order, as these two churches announce:

Calumet Park Covenant Church

Generally the poor are oppressed and locked out of the mainstream of our society. . . . God is calling us to open up opportunities to all who, as the Bible states, "Knock, Seek, Look." The Bible tells us we fight not against flesh and blood, but against evil rulers who seek through sin of pride and greed to keep others on the outside looking in.

Manchester Church of the Brethren

If war be sin, we believe that we are called to abolish war, for we . . . seek to listen obediently to Jesus. . . . "Blessed are the Peacemakers, for they shall be called the children of God" (Matt. 5.9). . . . Peace-making, for the Brethren, is . . . assertively seeking reconciliation and compassionate justice.

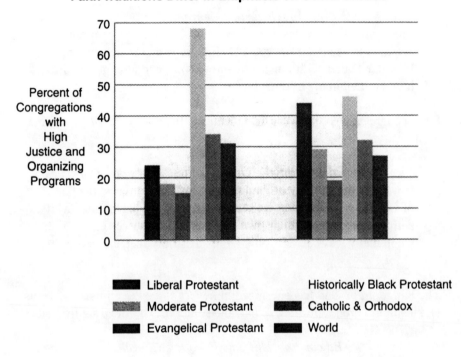

Figure 6.
Faith Traditions Differ in Emphasis on Social Justice

Percent of Congregations with High Justice and Organizing Programs

Liberal Protestant   Historically Black Protestant

Moderate Protestant   Catholic & Orthodox

Evangelical Protestant   World

"WE WALK WITH GOD'S PRESENCE"

Many churches recall how they have experienced God's presence with them in their ministries, but they use quite different images: Spirit, Jesus, Body of Christ, Kingdom of God, and an appeal to actions as more honest than words. This committee finds comfort in the Spirit of God's presence in every circumstance:

First Presbyterian Church, Canton
God not only created time, place, and us, but he is involved with us. . . . If it seems that our task is much too great for us . . . we are assured by the word that the Lord will be with us and that He is our strength. As found in Zechariah 4:6, "Not by might nor by power, but by my Spirit, says the Lord of Hosts."

For some groups, God is present in the Person of Jesus:

First Presbyterian Church, Canton
The church looks to Jesus in his relationship with the community.
We look to Jesus for the specific directions that he has given, to
love our Father with our heart, mind, soul, and strength, and to
love our neighbors as ourselves.

Some congregations emphasize their identity as the Body of Christ, continuing
his ministry:

Leet Memorial and Boyd's Grove United Methodist Churches
If we take the analogy of Paul concerning the church as the body
of Christ seriously, then we realize we dare not leave those who
suffer in any way to their own devices and resources either. For
we in many ways are His only hands, His only feet, and His only
voice.

The Kingdom of God has energized believers since the ministry of Jesus,
and it still has broad spiritual, social, and sometimes political significance:

Edwin Ray United Methodist Church
God's great compassion, or the Kingdom, has three aspects, inner,
beyond, and historical. . . . Our understanding of the call to social
ministry is founded on this perception of the Kingdom, where the
operating dynamic is love, and the character is peace and justice.
The church is attempting to give its community a glimpse of this
Kingdom.

An arrogant, condescending attitude can infect ministries where church
members come to feel that they alone have something to offer. Aware of
this risk, some congregations acknowledge that they learn and gain from
social ministries. In caring for others, they themselves are healed; in sharing
their faith, they find Christ already in the lives of the people with whom
they work:

South Chicago Covenant Church
An important basis for social ministry is to affirm that . . . all
people are loved by God. . . . The dignity and uniqueness of every

individual, the equality of all peoples, and our partnership in this life and on this world, all open us to acquaint ourselves with our neighbors, share in their struggles and their pain, and learn from them.

Some congregations act out their biblical faith more than they express it in the language of theology. They prefer to point to their actions rather than to articulate their faith:

Millard Congregational United Church of Christ
We are not a posturing church. We let our deeds do the talking. We are forever mindful that we are God's hands and feet on earth. We don't have to be God's mouth. We strive humbly to love by serving, to teach by doing, and to preach by being. That is our theology.

Despite the centrality of preaching for Pentecostal groups, the committee members at this Spirit-filled congregation sum up their faith simply:

Sweet Holy Spirit Baptist Church
Our church also follows a covenant that unites us to be mindful of how we walk, talk, and are seen by the world. We are the salt of the earth and a city that is placed on a hill that cannot be hid. Therefore we know that we must support missions abroad but never forget to impact our immediate community.

IDENTIFY THE LANGUAGE AND STYLE

Once you have settled on your sources, you should be able to identify the language and style of biblical tradition that pastors and members find persuasive. When you recognize the channels they are using, you can formulate your ministry in a way they will understand. Often in this exercise you need to discover the negative values of the church—what doesn't communicate—as much as what does. You may find that your church emphasizes creation or salvation, or embraces both. Some of the members of your church may want to respond to God's call in their freedom, and others may want the authority to feel they are commanded to respond. All churches feel the presence of God, but some images of presence fit more comfortably in your congregational tradition than others.

Find Sources in Your Heritage

Heritage provides the bridge between the timeless sources of faith, such as the Bible and the sacraments, and the particular experiences of faithfulness among the members of a congregation. It supports social ministry with a framework of values and commitments that are larger and older than the congregation itself. The affirmation of social ministry within that framework makes a program legitimate in the eyes of the local church; if we cannot show that affirmation, the program will remain suspect.

Church heritage is different from congregational history. History is what the congregation remembers from its own past. Heritage embraces a larger framing of the Christian faith, including the traditions and feelings that accrue to a congregation simply by belonging to a wider gathering of churches in the flow of Christian experience. History is the memory of the congregation, while heritage is the faith tradition they carry, which also carries them.

We find church heritage in many sources. We see it in official faith statements and policy papers and in churchwide patterns of organization and decision making. Names carry theological traditions—Baptist, Evangelical, Reformed, Unitarian-Universalist. Historic figures like Augustine, Aquinas, Luther, Calvin, and Wesley still impact our thinking. We can look at our architecture, examine our liturgy, listen to our music, read our creeds, observe our rituals, and talk with our historians; and yet heritage is always more intangible than any simple factual summary.

With this wealth of material available, you need to focus your search to make your study manageable. I suggest that you begin with the objective, official statements and move toward the more particular, personal stories. Your denomination's policy statements in areas that relate to your proposed ministry will be fairly accessible, and officials are generally pleased

II.3

**RESOURCES FOR
DENOMINATIONAL HISTORIES
AND STRATEGIES**

Davidson, James D., C. Lincoln Johnson, and Alan K. Mock. *Faith and Social Ministry: Ten Christian Perspectives.* Chicago: Loyola University Press, 1990.

Green, Clifford J. *Churches, Cities, and Human Community: Urban Ministry in the United States 1945-1985.* Grand Rapids: Eerdmans, 1996.

Villafane, Eldin. *Seek the Peace of the City: Reflections on Urban Ministry.* Grand Rapids: Eerdmans, 1995.

to be asked. Beyond those documents, I encourage you to look for ministries or actions of your wider church group that offer precedents (both structural and motivational) for your congregation to support your proposed program. Finally, I urge you to explore the stories of people in your own communion who have carried the faith in action and who symbolize the best of who you are.

Include three components, then, in your study of your church heritage: (a) examine church creeds and policy statements, (b) look for precedents in previous ministries, and (c) find the "saints" of the church.

CHURCH CREEDS AND POLICY STATEMENTS

Official church statements give permission and encouragement for local congregations to become involved in social ministry. The documents provide a tangible link between the issues facing the congregation and the social traditions of the church. A Methodist church takes pride in its pioneering church policy:

> *Leet Memorial and Boyd's Grove United Methodist Churches*
> In 1910, the Methodist Church became the first denomination to draft a social creed in which we find these words: "We believe in the right and duty of persons to work for . . . the elimination of economic and social distress."

Catholic parishes often cite the more recent pastoral epistles of the United States Conference of Bishops:

St. Joan of Arc Catholic Church
In the recent U.S. Bishops' pastoral entitled "Economic Justice for All," we see expressed the heart of the Church in its option for the poor: "We feel the pain of our sisters and brothers who are poor, unemployed, homeless, living on the edge—it summons the Church also to be an instrument in assisting people to experience the liberating power of God in their own lives, so that they may respond to the gospel in freedom and dignity."

Although these historic statements may help when you need board approval, fund raising, or other official sanctions, most congregations use official statements sparingly or not at all. To gain wide support for the ministry among your parishioners, the other, less formal elements of heritage will be more powerful.

Planning committees often find support for community ministries by citing previous activities and continuing programs that document their denominational commitment to social ministry. Typically a Methodist church will trace its roots back to ministries among working-class people in England and the United States:

Irvington United Methodist Church
Early Methodists developed schools, clinics, programs for the aged, and even cottage industries for unemployed. Their view of Christian discipleship called for giving food to the hungry, clothing to the naked, visiting or helping those sick or in prison. This tendency continues in the American church.

The Church of the Brethren, the Mennonites, and other pietist movements have a particular historical consciousness carried by—and carrying—a community with distinctive faith commitments. In choosing a pacifist interpretation of the gospel, they align themselves with people who are persecuted and pushed to the margins of society. This Brethren church is well aware of its heritage as a basis for social ministry:

Church of the Brethren, Manchester
Persecution in Europe resulted in many members migrating to America from 1719 to 1729 in search of religious and economic freedom. The Brethren refused to serve in the Revolutionary War

and moved farther into the wilderness, including Maryland and
Virginia. There they gained their livelihood from the soil, lived at
peace with the Indians, and established new churches. At the
time of the Civil War the Brethren lived in both the North and
South. Some draftees served, others hired substitutes or sought
asylum in the North or in Free Territory. Others sought to reconcile
differences, resulting in persecution, economic hardship, and
martyrdom. Conscientious objectors were sent to prison or granted
a noncombatant status during WWI. Alternative service was an
additional option during WWII. . . . As an historical peace church,
these convictions have led members into worldwide ventures and
volunteer service for promoting peace.

For most congregations, denominational heritage is not constricting but
liberating as a basic platform on which to build community outreach programs.
As you work through this study, you are laying a foundation that moves
from policies to ministries—from the abstractions of faith statements to the
embodiment of faith actions.

"Saints" of the Church

Planning committees in Catholic parishes rarely use the precedent of
churchwide ministry programs to claim their heritage of social ministry.
Most often they use the lives of saints. Catholics always have stories and
events around individuals who embody the caring qualities of the faith. This
congregation's statement is typical of many:

St. Mary's Catholic Church, Alexandria
There are many stories of countless numbers of saints who have
given and helped the needy and the poor. St. Vincent DePaul is
one known to many for his quiet way of knocking on the door of
the poor, offering them help here and now, and then leaving silently.
. . . No fuss, no muss, no embarrassing questions or case number,
just help, share, and love unselfishly. Pope Gregory was another
person in our heritage who urged and brought about . . . land
reforms for the more humane treatment of servants and tenant
farmers. . . . Mother Teresa of Calcutta, known all over the world

today, speaks and demonstrates the attitudes of social caring and sharing we as a church wish to express.

Often the name of the parish embodies a congregation's identity. This city church has been working toward a ministry with youth:

St. Joan of Arc Catholic Church

Our name-saint, Joan of Arc, was a simple peasant girl who was "of the people," rather than "of the organization." She was a champion of the "Will of God." She was a woman of action; she held a grand disdain for obstacles, whether major or minor, that blocked her path. . . . Joan was [a] youth. She was scarcely 18 when she raised the siege of Orleans. Joan is youth. Joan, the Maid, remains with us today as a model of courage and maidenly virtue in a world so much in need of her example.

Some Protestants also find a sense of Christian caring embodied in the name of a congregation:

St. Luke's United Methodist Church

When the United Brethren and Evangelical United Brethren Church [two predecessor bodies of the United Methodist Church] combined, they renamed themselves St. Luke's Evangelical United Brethren Church. There are two implications in the name they selected. First, St. Luke was a physician—a loving and caring person who helped others. Secondly, United Brethren implies a group of people joining together to help their fellow man (brethren). Social concern and ministry could therefore be considered a natural extension of St. Luke's name.

Although the Protestant Reformation made a theological point of denying a unique status to selected saints, contemporary Protestants readily name heroic figures who embody their beliefs. When asked to identify "a symbolic leader of your faith who has influenced you in developing social ministries," the church leaders we work with most frequently point to Martin Luther King, Jr., and Pope John XXIII.

In addition, each Protestant denomination can name champions who have made an impact within that communion, but who rarely find much following outside. This Protestant pantheon tends to include significant theological leaders who have emerged at an important juncture in the life of the church. Catholics, on the other hand, rarely confuse the wisdom of theologians with the piety of saints.

In their search for identity, Presbyterians turn first to the Swiss theologian-reformer John Calvin and American pastor-patriot John Witherspoon:

> *Hope Presbyterian Church*
> John Calvin not only preached the gospel of salvation, but a gospel of social responsibility. . . . John Witherspoon signed the Declaration of Independence as his ministerial commitment to justice and freedom. . . . Our history is replete with persons who have been on the frontiers of all major social issues.

Baptist churches find a spiritual ancestor in the early American fight for religious freedom by Roger Williams and in a theologian-activist from the turn of the century:

> *Baptist Temple*
> Walter Rauschenbusch is credited by some to be among the first proponents of the social gospel. As a Baptist pastor in New York's "Hell's Kitchen" in the late 19th century, Rauschenbusch saw the need . . . for better housing, better working conditions, and the elimination of disease and crime.

DRAWING UPON PAST SAINTS

You may find the key to locating the saints of the church in the way the Methodists treat the Wesleys. Every Methodist church seems to remember Methodism's founders, but each for a different reason, according to its own situation. For example, a church in a rural town recalls how John and Charles Wesley preached "the Good News in small towns and rural areas like ours," while a more urban congregation with a strong educational program remembers that John Wesley "founded schools because he realized the importance of education." You cannot simply mold the lives of great leaders to fit the needs of a local situation, but the giants of the faith offer a rich variety of stories of commitment for us to draw upon as we shape our ministries. In drawing on past saints, you suggest a longevity of commitment to ministry, which you invite the present membership to continue.

Build on Your Congregational History

History is not the dead past, but the strengths and softness, the confidence and weakness, the heroes and the hidden bodies that a congregation carries from previous experience. Such history has many sources. Creeds might be described as the resolution of former theological disputes, and rituals reenact once-controversial decisions about faith, authority, and the meaning of membership in this congregation. The architecture, pictures, and symbols that adorn the church offer public witness to the historic identity of the congregation. The hymns and special music, the prayers and liturgy, the offering received and the sacraments celebrated, the announcements and rubrics of worship, the roles of clergy and laity—all are elements of the congregation's history enacted in the present. Congregational history is everywhere and inescapable.

Church stories, however, are the most accessible carriers of history. We are interested in the stories of people and events that are remembered and shared in congregational life. Sometimes we hear these stories in formal situations, but more likely we discover them in conversational gossip. These can be

---

II.4

RESOURCES FOR MOBILIZING CONGREGATIONAL STORIES

Dudley, Carl, and Sally A. Johnson. *Energizing the Congregation: Images that Shape Your Church's Ministry.* Louisville: Westminster John Knox. 1993.

Gillespie, Joanna Bowen, *Women Speak of God, Congregations and Chamge.* Philadephia: Trinity Press International, 1995.

Wimberly, Edward. *Recalling Our Own Stories.* San Francisco: Jossey-Bass, 1997.

funny and pointed at the same time, when humorous memories carry hard values to challenge membership commitments. These stories also surface in a decision-making crisis, providing models for choices and energy for sealing the choice with action.

The stories live because they show us what is authentic in the congregation. Sometimes they guide us like a rudder through hard times. Often they confirm a sense of belonging—for those who tell them and those who listen. Stories help us incorporate outsiders who want to join the church, as we invite them to listen and to add a story of their own. Stories may be used for discipline and guidance, recalling the past to affirm or challenge the beliefs or behavior of the present. For the purpose of this study, we will look at the stories that connect the congregation with prior experiences in social ministry.

Listen for the stories that the congregation remembers and retells. For many members, especially the older ones, these are the foundations on which the church is built. They are retold at celebrations, in times of decision, in moments of consolation, and in other transitional experiences. We recount these memories of significant events and people to give ballast and direction to congregational identity in moments of uncertainty and change. These stories bring a variety of emotions—humor for their human failings, anger for decisions that now inhibit our choices, reverence for sacrifice in behalf of lofty ideals, and commitment to maintain a continuity with their remembered greatness.

As your committee seeks to mobilize your congregation for social ministry, collect your significant stories: who are you as a church, how you got there, and how you relate to your community. You should not force your stories through any prescribed theme or design, but look for the images that reflect congregational identity and therefore mobilize the energy of your congregation.

In my experience, church stories cluster around some broad characteristic themes, which churches mix and match in the retelling of their stories. As examples of the way focused images can mobilize churches, we clustered these mini-stories around five basic themes by which congregations link their histories to social ministries:

- Journey stories of ethnic-cultural congregations;
- Crisis stories of churches that struggle for survival;
- Rooted stories with a place for spiritual growth;

- Service stories of caring for people; and
- Mission stories of vision for a better world.

JOURNEY STORIES OF ETHNIC-CULTURAL CONGREGATIONS

The earliest memories have roots in other countries, most frequently the old European nations. Sometimes these are told from the perspective of those who came and sometimes from the viewpoint of those who welcomed the newcomer. The first example comes from a Hispanic congregation that remembers two previous waves of migration. In these few words they project their own experiences into previous generations ("We've always been this way") and tell a story their denomination also finds appealing:

> *Millard Congregational United Church of Christ*
> From its inception our church was an oasis welcoming those people whom other established churches were reluctant to accept into their fold. The early membership consisted of the newly arrived Bohemians who did not fit the requirements of the existing local churches. Later on, it consisted of displaced Appalachian whites who were attracted by the social gospel preached and practiced even in those early years. We acted in accordance with the teachings of Jesus, striving to meet successfully the test of true fellowship.

Another church makes an explicit connection between the challenges of the past and the ministry they are now developing:

> *Douglas Park Covenant Church*
> From the very beginning, education of their children was of concern to the parents in the immigrant section. The first call to a permanent pastor stipulated that he should conduct a school. . . . Education [was] the church's focus for the next half-century, with a sensitivity to the new families who arrived jobless, homeless, and rootless. . . . In the 1960s, our community ethnic composition changed as Hispanics became the predominant group. In 1972 the Spanish ministry began . . . with an emphasis on education.

Two Lutheran churches, one Swedish American and one Chinese American, weave their stories together as they plan a shared ministry of education and employment for recent Chinese immigrants:

Immanuel Lutheran Church

The early Immanuel Lutheran Church ministered to a congregation of Swedish immigrants who found themselves in straitened circumstances. They lived in shanties or in other crowded rented dwellings. . . . A cholera epidemic in 1854 and a failure of most banks added to their privations. Through all of this the church helped its members find jobs, learn the language, and adapt to the culture and surroundings of their new homeland. Many of the Chinese Church congregation endured long and dangerous pilgrimages to freedom in this country. Their stories of the hardships parallel those of Immanuel's early members. The Chinese Church's ministry to the spiritual and social needs of today's immigrants is repeating Immanuel's early ministry to the Swedish immigrants.

CRISIS STORIES OF CHURCHES THAT STRUGGLE FOR SURVIVAL

An even more common theme in congregational history revolves around hardship and struggle. In many ways the hard times may be more useful than the comfortable experiences. In these challenges we test our values and commitments—the stuff that gives us our identity and keeps us together when the pressure is less severe. For many congregations the memories of the crises they have survived nourish the muscle of their faith.

Some churches have memories of oppression, survival, and acceptance that set the stage for ministries with other newcomers today. This brief but poignant comment from a comparatively wealthy Catholic parish reminds the congregation of its history:

St. Joan of Arc Catholic Church

The Ku Klux Klan was active in Indiana in the '20s. Catholic and foreign-born families often felt unwelcome in the inner city. They found comfort under the wing of St. Joan of Arc Church.

The memory of financial struggles often shapes the character of the church. Churches can use their stories of hardship and commitment to reclaim their character and mobilize their energies for ministry a generation later.

Irvington United Methodist Church

From the beginning, funding was a struggle. A tithing band, projects by the women such as weekly peanut sales, kept the church afloat. When the depression of the 1930s came, the church was literally saved from bankruptcy by a few families who mortgaged their homes to get cash to make payments on the debt. . . . [During this time the church began] an early and centering ministry in the Marion County Children's Guardian Home. Church women provided Christmas gifts, furnished supplies, mended clothing, and taught a church school class. The church still provides similar support.

Another congregation names its decades by the nature of the struggle in which the church is engaged. This story is unusually frank about the gains and losses in their struggle for survival:

Martin Temple AME Zion Church

The first 10 years in the life of this congregation, as expressed by those who know it best, is described as a "Decade in the Desert" . . . "Years of Yearning." . . . The young struggling congregation moved from a bus garage to an American Legion Post to a funeral home to a borrowed Apostolic church. Even then, however, this People of God had dreams and visions. . . .

The arrival of Reverend Fisher marked the beginning of the next decade in our history. He found the situation very bleak. The membership, which was never very large, had dwindled; the notes of more than $900.00 per month were due, and the church was over $90,000 in debt. This overwhelming indebtedness, more than anything else, shaped this period labeled "Decade of Debt." Current members from this era still speak of fish fries, chicken dinners, the devil's funeral, and other lucrative and not-so-lucrative enterprises. . . . All energy, so it seemed, was spent on fund raising; but the people had a mind to work. . . .

The decade ended with the church debt-free and with a membership on roll of nearly 400 people. . . . In the battle against the debt, many casualties occurred. Relationships were strained, families were divided, members left and members became inactive, but the church moved on. The two years following the mortgage burning were years of celebration and transition. The people were pausing to catch their breath.

Sometimes deep emotions create a significant gap between the historical events and congregational memories. In the tensions of these congregations, we can recall that the openness of congregations toward racial/ethnic change is in direct proportion to their previous experience with cross-cultural diversity (see fig. 7).

Figure 7.
Location Makes a Difference in Racial/Ethnic Diversity

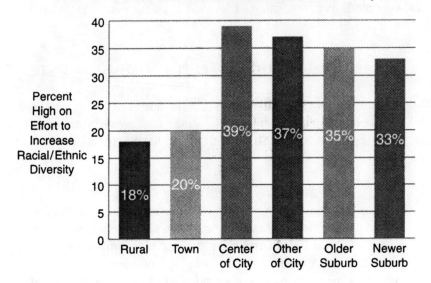

Another African American congregation tells a vivid story of racial transition. While the facts are in dispute, the character of their memory is a powerful and sad reality:

Zion Community Church

As the white flight accelerated, members left the church, never to come back. Most members moved out of the neighborhood. As membership was decreasing, the black members noticed it and saw no alternative but to try and buy the church. . . . After a bitter struggle, the black members were successful in purchasing the church. The white members took all the funds and records, and left the church with a mortgage, two pastors, and seven black members. "It was like a rapture had taken place," stated one of the members who witnessed the ordeal.

Although the details of historical fact in such a story are open to challenge (for example, no records were lost, no property sold), the account demonstrates the power of memory to shape identity and mobilize energy; it also reminds us to confirm the historical basis for the stories we tell.

ROOTED STORIES WITH A PLACE FOR SPIRITUAL GROWTH

Many churches root their identity in rich memories of places where they have experienced significant events. Place and memory are attached, and congregations will sacrifice mightily to have a space they can call their own:

Sweet Holy Spirit Baptist Church

[When the church] outgrew her previous location, regardless of the existing financial situation we were able to acquire a new church on West 103rd Street. This "renovated storefront building" was certainly a blessing regardless of the problems therein. We needed a roof, a furnace, and so much more, but with prayer and faith, along with the faithful contributions of the people, God did just what he said he would do!

Some churches see their buildings as more than just a shelter for the congregation; they also offer it as a home for a variety of community activities. These groups find strength both in claiming their space and in offering it to others. These congregations have no sharp line between church members and community residents; they have a parish sense of ministry:

Community United Church of Christ

For well over 125 years our congregation functioned as a nondenominational community church, and the sense of being "community" remains extremely strong. Our founders established a place for people in the community to meet and share their faith as well as their sense of mission. . . . In providing a home for our faith, we are also providing a place for the expression of that faith through service and availability to the wider community.

SERVICE STORIES OF CARING FOR PEOPLE

One virtually universal story retells the way members care for other members in times of danger, hardship, illness, and transitions of all sorts. These memories tend to take two very different forms, which have a significant impact on the development of social ministry. In the first story the church takes pride in the way it looks after its own people:

Sweet Holy Spirit Baptist Church

We have no record of organized charities in the beginning, but there must have been the usual "rectory door" variety. Sewing circles made not only baptismal gowns and first Communion dresses, but also clothing and bedding for the poor. Women's Club and Legion of Mary members visited the sick and assisted families in time of bereavement. These works were, however, primarily within the parish membership.

The other story reflects a concern for others beyond the membership of the church. By carrying such a memory, this church more easily accepts a ministry beyond present membership and more quickly joins with other churches in developing that ministry. Note also how the memory serves to reinforce in their congregational identity that "we've always done" these things:

Leet Memorial and Boyd's Grove United Methodist Churches

The congregation has always been evangelistic as well as mission-minded. Truckloads of corn have been sent for CROP as well as rabbits and chickens to migrant farmworkers' camps in the area.

During the twenties and thirties the women canned fruit and the youth gathered canned goods, soap, towels, wash clothes, toothbrushes and paste for the Methodist Hospital in Peoria.

Some churches look not only to the past, but also to the future, seeing service as a new story in which they themselves can be changed even as they reach out to help others:

St. Mary's Catholic Church, Alexandria
It is very difficult and a very slow process to get people once again revitalized and remotivated. This is why [a ministry project] is so important to us. We need a project of social outreach, a program in which we can reach out to each other and to the community and become an ecumenical source of hope to all people in this small community.

MISSION STORIES OF VISION FOR A BETTER WORLD

Some congregations look back on a history of addressing broad community problems. They seek to work with the larger institutional systems that affect the lives of everyone, and they try to change the causes of the problems people face. This church group recalls a strategy of moving from contact to awareness, from providing services to making policy:

Washington Street Presbyterian Church
Recently the church divided the neigh-borhood into seven districts, assigning an elder and deacon to each district. They were responsible for keeping tabs on community activities and events: illness, deaths, etc., of neighborhood residents as well as church members. . . . Since that time we have developed a food pantry, English classes for Asian refugees, monthly rummage sales, a recreation program for elementary school . . . children, H.O.M.E. (a house painting project), a quarterly community newsletter, and active involvement on the boards of nearly all neighborhood multiservice centers, community, business, and ministerial associations.

Congregations may find their identity in advocating and modeling innovative programs that the community might adopt and institutionalize. In the story of this church, the focus is not on the program itself but on how it influenced others:

Westminster Presbyterian Church

Concern for children is characteristic of this congregation. Westminster has housed and/or sponsored a variety of programs for children, including tutoring, nursery schools, a school for gifted children of color, and a child development center for the children of migrant workers. The tutoring program later became a model for a district-wide project for the city. . . . Our facility has always provided a forum and meeting place for community groups. We feel it is our opportunity to show that we believe in the unity of all God's creatures.

II.5
RESOURCES FOR
RECORDING CONGREGATIONAL
STORIES

Claman, Victor N., and David E. Butler. *Acting On Your Faith: Congregations Making a Difference.* Boston: Insights, 1994.

Friedman, Samuel G. *Upon This Rock: The Miracles of a Black Church.* New York: HarperCollins, 1993.

Wilkes, Paul. *Excellent Catholic Parishes: The Guide to Best Places and Practices.* New York: Paulist, 2001.

———. *Excellent Protestant Congregations: The Guide to Best Places and Practices.* Louisville: Westminser John Knox, 2001.

Sometimes social involvement in one era gives permission for new programs in another. From its large neo-gothic exterior and relatively wealthy membership, you would not expect this congregation to hire a community organizer for social change—unless you knew this fragment of their story:

First Meridian Heights Presbyterian Church
A century ago the Social Gospel Movement and the United Way were expressions of a common concern. . . . They started prison reform, made treatment of the mentally ill more humane, began day-care centers, organized programs to help immigrants make a

new home in America, and created public health departments and juvenile courts. . . . Our church was a leader of the Social Gospel Movement.

HISTORY AS ALLY

History can be your ally and resource in mobilizing your congregation for social ministry when you find precedents for commitment and when you get inside the logic of the stories the congregation tells. Enjoy your search for stories, knowing how they can help release and focus the energy of the congregation through ministry.

Analyze Strengths and Limitations through a Survey

We previously explored the triangle of insights that interact to shape the congregation's identity in social ministry: Scripture, tradition, and experience. By now you have gathered a variety of material on your church's triangle of biblical foundations, Christian heritage, and particular history. These form the building blocks to understand how social ministry fits within your identity and to develop congregational support for your ministry.

Every few years you may wish to go the second mile beyond the leadership of the church to hear what a broadly based sample of church members thinks, feels, and believes. Your membership survey can be brief or extensive, highly focused or wide in scope, written or oral, done individually or in groups. Whatever your method and content, as church leaders your views are likely to be generally affirmed—but you may also be surprised in several significant areas. I use a membership survey frequently because support for social ministry is an area in which leaders tend to be less accurate about the beliefs and commitments of church members.

You may choose a written questionnaire that invites members to express their views within previously determined categories of response; this approach enables you to compare the views of members throughout your congregation. A questionnaire covers a wide variety of information on the members' values and commitments, including questions of congregational identity, biblical faith, and the relationship between the church and its social context.

A membership survey gives you a different perspective for understanding your congregation. Much of your study of biblical foundations, church heritage, and congregational history reflects the insights and memories of church leaders, but a survey draws on a much larger base. You have summarized your work in Steps 1, 2, and 3 in brief narrative reports, and you may have discussed the reports with groups in the church. The survey, however, provides a statistical report and makes its impact by showing the popularity of particular views. The survey also has its limits: We may know how many people supported a particular view, but we do not know how important the question is to them. The survey gives extensive, measured information (see fig. 8), while narrative gives more depth and a measure of intensity.

Figure 8.
Faith Traditions Differ in Number of Social Ministries

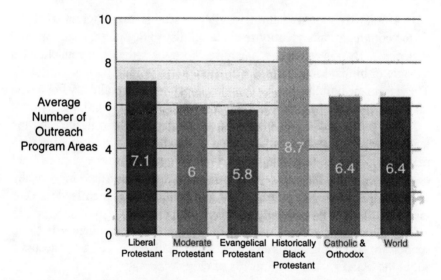

I suggest that you plan your survey well in advance of the time you would like to share the results. Several excellent church membership surveys are available from denominational offices, seminaries, and consultants. You can design your own survey from existing material, such as the questionnaire published in the appendix of *Studying Congregations: A New Handbook*, by Nancy T. Ammerman, et al. (Nashville: Abingdon, 1998), or *Rural Congregational Studies: A Guide for Good Shepherds*, by L. Shannon Jung (Nashville: Abingdon, 1997).

Your survey offers a larger framework for understanding the personal commitments and social dynamics of congregational life. As such, it will help you to look first at the profile of a single congregation and then to compare your results with information from other congregations. Ideally, the most stimulating educational environment for learning from a survey is a group of churches that use the same questionnaire and then discuss the results together.

Of the extensive data you can gain about your members' perspectives and the dynamics of your church, here we focus on some of the kinds of information you can learn about your congregational identity. I have organized the examples from churches around several basic questions that may concern you as you seek support and commitment for your social ministry program:

- Context: What is the relationship of our church to its community?
- Identity: What is our members' sense of congregational unity?
- Trust: How have members responded to our decision making?
- Faith: Does the faith of our church support this ministry?
- Commitment: Will our members give to support this ministry?
- Advocacy: Should justice be a primary focus of our ministry?

CONTEXT

The social sensitivity of a few leaders guides most congregations. They have little information about the way the majority of members feel about the church and even less about how they are seen in the community. Thus churches seize upon the information that helps a congregation see itself in relation to its community, as this church reports:

Community United Church of Christ
We are seen in our community as ecumenical, "open," liberal, community-minded, autonomous, tolerant, and cooperative. We see ourselves as a caring and committed community of Christians, seeking to follow the call to mission in a variety of styles and programs.

Another church discovered a genuine liability in the congregation's efforts to develop an educational outreach by church volunteers working with community people:

First Meridian Heights Presbyterian Church
The education of the average member may make it difficult to
relate effectively with the very people with whom the project
seeks to work. . . . [However] the education of the congregation
does indicate an interest in education, which suggests that an issue
related to education would be supported.

This church discovered the same distance between congregation and
community, but converted the gap into an opportunity:

North United Methodist Church
Although North Church prides itself on diversity of opinion, theology,
and interests, it has become evident through the membership survey
that we are very homogeneous in regard to race, educational level,
and to a slightly lesser degree socioeconomic status. Thus, we
have a great deal to learn from our community.

IDENTITY

Since most congregational leaders emphasize the familial images of the
church as "home" and the members as "family," they are often shocked to
discover that many members see the church quite differently. Members in
this church feel themselves to be religious without a need for intimacy; they
see the church as a gathering of caring individuals, loosely knit but ready to
help when needed:

Baptist Temple
Personal, individual religion is our focus; 78 percent pray every
day. . . . But this personal, individual style of religion results in a
low sense of church family; 38 percent have no close friends in
the congregation. . . . The membership thus seems to work better
together as individuals than as groups.

This church also recognizes the loss of the family image, but sees in
mutual help an opportunity for unity:

First Presbyterian Church, Canton

We are not so much a family at this time as we are a mini-community, a more loosely knit association of individuals and groups . . . [in which] we overwhelmingly agree (83 percent) that our members help each other out in times of trouble.

A survey can help us discover diversity within the congregation. Finding these subgroups among us may be a difficult experience; some discoveries confirm our fears, while others offer unexpected opportunity:

St. Boniface Catholic Church

We are now aware that there is a definite subgroup in the congregation that will not be cooperative and [that] speaks strongly against the project.

We identified a surprising subgroup within our congregation . . . [that] believe in the local community and are willing to give their money to support the church. . . . We will have to make a specific effort to personally reach out to this subgroup to involve them in our ministry project.

TRUST

Your committee can learn a good deal from survey questions in which members comment on congregational goals, conflicts, and decision making. For one group, the survey shows a general affirmation of their decision making but suggests an area for future concern:

Hope Presbyterian Church

The membership survey tends to validate the process we employed to arrive at a decision concerning our ministry project. It also validates what we thought the home meetings revealed about our corporate personality, about our understanding of the worship-mission relationship, and about our willingness to be involved in social ministry. . . . On the other hand . . . it may be somewhat difficult for us to relinquish some of the control over the project and to give our partners as much flexibility as they may need.

FAITH

Many church leaders find that to challenge the congregation to respond to community needs they must draw on the faith commitments of members who have little available time. This urban parish puts into words what many others have said, thought, and prayed:

> *St. Mary's Catholic Church, Indianapolis*
> The surveyed members answered that they perceived their church as being involved in activities of social services, but have responded that they had no time to assist in such services. Sixty-nine percent indicated that the pastor speaks . . . on the need to be involved in social outreach. Apparently what is heard by the congregation does not move them to action. The congregation sees itself as a fairly religious group, and this was supported by other data. . . . So the potential for giving and sharing is there in the congregation. How to unleash that powerful action is the challenge.

If congregational leaders believe they are more concerned about the community than the average church member, the results of a survey may be surprising. The survey allows many new voices to speak out, sometimes from neglected corners of the congregation:

> *St. Joan of Arc Catholic Church*
> The survey reports that St. Joan Church is, indeed, motivated and inspired by its Catholic-Christian faith to work for social outreach. Seventy-four percent of our congregation said that their faith makes them want to work to eliminate injustice, poverty, and hunger. Thirty-nine percent said they volunteer in community ministries once a month or more.

COMMITMENT

Most churches face a clear gap between the members' faith commitments and their actual involvement in ministry. This congregation combined their discoveries of a problem and their strategy for response:

St. Thomas Aquinas Catholic Church

The implications of these responses are twofold: First, we need to design the volunteer roles in our project so that people in the parish believe that they have the lime and talent to do them; and second, given that most of our parishioners attend Sunday worship, we need to incorporate aspects of our ministry project in the worship services, highlighting the importance of this ministry and the need for the parishioners to get involved in it. If our parish clergy promote it, our members will respond.

Through a survey your committee can assess the mood of the congregation—how it feels about itself and how the new ministry may fit into the faith and life of the membership. This church weaves faith and feelings together to help members gain strength from developing a program to improve their community:

Washington Street Presbyterian Church

From the membership survey, we learned that we bring many strengths to a potential project. Our congregation has a very high morale and positive outlook for the community's future. There is a strong sense of identification with our present community ministries. . . . Eighty-three percent of the respondents agreed that volunteering to help others is an expression of faith, and 74 percent said that their faith makes them want to eliminate poverty and hunger. [In fact] 30 percent already volunteer in our community ministries.

ADVOCACY

Perhaps the most difficult discussions (and decisions) about social ministries arise from the conflict between those who want to provide ministries of service to people in need and those who want to undertake justice ministries for systemic change. A membership survey cannot resolve the question, but it will map the terrain for you, making the challenge very clear:

St. Mary's Catholic Church, Alexandria
[Congregational values and] leadership roles tend to be more in
the areas of finance, education, and the social life of the parish,
than in mission and social justice.

However, in some congregations you will find strong support for
ministries that care about people and that are committed to changing unjust
conditions:

Washington Street Presbyterian Church
We understand that since we worship a God of justice, we should
try to be just in our daily lives. Programs to help the needy were
ranked equally with worship as the highest priority for our church.

Finally, this example shows the challenge a Catholic parish finds in its
membership survey and the way it uses the strengths of Christian identity,
weaving together the elements of history, tradition, and biblical faith into a
more meaningful social ministry:

St. Thomas Aquinas Catholic Church
Finally in examining identity, 29 percent indicated that the church
should work for "justice" by working to end inequality and
oppression, while 54 percent interpreted the "God of justice" on a
personal level, such as being fair in personal dealings. Clearly this
demonstrates that we must educate the parishioners more
completely on the social teachings of the Catholic Church so that
they understand the justice advocacy component of our ministry
as coming from our religious tradition.

MAPPING THE TERRAIN

One measure of your leadership is your sensitivity to the views of members
throughout the congregation—but leadership is more than reading the opinion
polls. The survey offers you an instrument for listening to a wider selection
of voices focused on particular questions and responding at the same time.
The results map the terrain, but they do not tell you the route to be taken.

After listening, leaders must make decisions based on their own convictions about what God expects of us in particular situations.

We have noted briefly the kinds of information a survey might offer in response to questions of the church in its context and the members' views of congregational unity, confidence in decision making, faith in social ministry, time for volunteering, and understanding of social advocacy. You may wish to ask other questions that push the church or challenge its unity. Membership surveys, when planned and used sparingly, can inform church leaders and members, show a profile of large and small groups within the congregation, and lay the groundwork for self-understanding and stronger social ministry.

CHECKLIST FOR PART II:

Congregational Identity

Step 1: Identity Your Biblical Foundations. (pp. 68-76)

We have identified key biblical pasages and faith traditions that describe our foundational reasons for community ministry.
Date: _____   *Assigned to:*_____

Step 2: Find Sources in Your Heritage (pp.77-83)

We have reviewed key creeds, confessions, and denominational policy statements that support community ministry.
Date: _____   *Assigned to:*_____

We have reviewed our congregation's past to learn about precedents in community ministry.
Date: _____   *Assigned to:* _____

We have recalled "saints, heroes, and giants of the faith" in our local and wider tradition, who have pioneered community ministries.
Date: _____   *Assigned to:* _____

Step 3: Build on Your Congregational History (pp. 84-94)

We have noted the stories of (especially our older) members and examined our church's history for key themes that have guided our faith in serving neighbors and communities.
Date: _____   *Assigned to:* _____

Step 4: Analyze Your Strengths and Limitations (pp. 95-103)

We have conducted a congregational survey and tabulated the results..
Date: _____   *Assigned to:* _____

We have summarized our findings in congregational identity in one or more brief statements, and made these known the the congregation.
Date: _____   *Assigned to:* _____

We have reviewed our ministry focus (Part I) in light of all we've learned in Part II.
Date: _____   *Assigned to:* _____

Organizing for Social Ministry

Organizing for Social Ministry

All churches rely on the same foundations in mobilizing for social ministry. When congregations get beyond "familiarity blindness" to rediscover their turf, then they can focus on genuine options in community ministry. Congregations that link their social ministry with their Christian identity and congregational culture have access to renewable energy: They know what they want to do, and why they want to do it. The prerequisites for organizing are community awareness and membership commitment—in faith.

Social ministries have a high correlation with congregational vitality, as evident in the dramatic differences shown in the FACT report on over 14,000 congregations in 41 faith communities (see fig. 9). Although there is no evidence that clients join the congregations where these ministries are located, social outreach and a concern for social justice appear to have a positive impact on congregational participation. But various congregations organize around different issues, and they organize for these ministries in their own ways. With wide differences among congregations in heritage, polity, styles, culture, resources, and leadership styles, a single pattern of organization would be impossible. In our common concern for social ministry, the way we mobilize in each congregation is unique to the people involved and the problems they face.

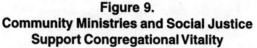

Figure 9.
Community Ministries and Social Justice
Support Congregational Vitality

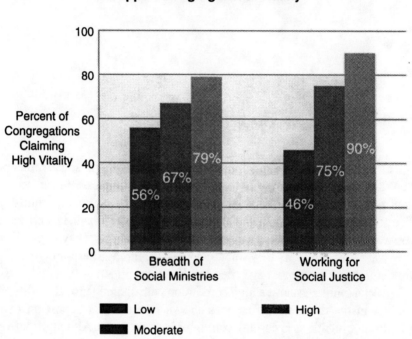

Organizing puts ideas on wheels, translates faith into action, and enables our vision for ministry to become a tangible reality. If we think of social context as the air we breathe and identity as the soul or center of our being, then organization is the bone and decision making is the muscle that makes things happen. Organizing:

- clarifies our purposes during the struggle to achieve them;
- shows the depth and duration of our commitment;
- demands fresh resources and generates new energy;
- challenges narrow ideas and expands our experience;
- shapes our perceptions even as we shape the program;
- breaks old stereotypes and builds new alliances; and
- helps us touch the lives of others and be touched in return.

For all these reasons, we should be more delighted when our organization succeeds than dismayed when it fails. Organizing is more than mechanical effort—it transforms us in the process.

An organization is not a fixed structure but a dynamic relationship among a group of people who have agreed to work for a common goal through separate tasks. We can make an organizational chart by mapping out the tasks, the people, and their relationships to one another. But there are no right answers, no clear-cut guidelines to measure the chart's correctness. We can measure the effectiveness of an organization only against the goals it has established (and revised as needed), conditioned by the problems it has faced in working toward those goals.

The task of organizing is a puzzle to be solved, not a blueprint to be followed. In this part, I will discuss and give examples of the ways congregations have handled several significant elements that you will face as you begin to organize your social ministry. How will you fit the social ministry into the existing congregational management style? How will you hold a common vision, yet accomplish each step along the way? How will you expand your base without losing your constituency? How will your ministry empower the people you are trying to serve? Although the styles of organizing differ, the result is similar— that is, community programs that are well organized and clear in their purposes can make a marked contribution to congregational life and encourage membership growth. Organizing is worth doing, and doing well.

Basic elements of organizing are grouped into four steps of foundational work for even the simplest ministries. Although steps in earlier sections can be worked on separately, typically these are engaged concurrently—as you work on one, another will appear and need attention. In Part IV we will discuss related areas essential to expand your ministry. Each of these is hard work, but also energizing as your ministry reflects the transforming power of the God's Spirit moving in and through your work.

III.1
RESOURCES FOR ORGANIZING CASE HISTORIES FROM RURAL AND URBAN MINISTRIES

Hinsdale, Mary Ann, Helen M. Lewis, and S. Maxine Waller. *It Comes from the People: Community Development and Local Theology.* Philadelphia: Temple University Press, 1995.

Woodson, Robert. *The Triumphs of Joseph.* New York: Free Press, 1998.

Step 1. Build Organization

At the core of your ministry is a leadership group and style that affirms your purpose in your setting, granting appropriate authority and resources to act.

Step 2. Develop Volunteers

Finding, training, incorporating, and supporting volunteers to get the most from your ministry is your most demanding and relentless challenge.

Step 3. Share Ministry

Since social ministries affect all participants, leaders must include consumers in a shared commitment to mutual healing and transformation.

Step 4. Focus Your Ministry

Recognizing a natural tension between compassion and justice, leaders must intentionally focus their ministry in ways that generate positive energy.

Build Organization:
Authority through Authenticity

ere is the organizational challenge: Your authority for social ministry is based on a combination of compassion for people in need (and anger about systems that need changing) and the resources available in your situation. Your study of the social context should have demonstrated a need for your ministry that you can state with force and clarity. But the shape and dynamics of the organization are always a compromise between the urgent community needs and all the baggage of congregational memories and community experiences. These memories and experiences are usually ambiguous, unstated, and sometimes even conflicting.

Overtly, social ministry organization grows from the statement of need. As an organizer, however, you recognize that the opening statement of ministry is only half of the organizational rationale. The rest involves negotiating among individual and community values until you find the form of management that feels right to the people involved. It is never as simple as "form follows function." Those from the trenches explain the alternatives.

> **III.2**
> **RESOURCES FOR**
> **ORGANIZATION BUILDING**
>
> Cheyne, John. *Incarnational Agents: A Guide to Development Ministries.* Birmingham, Ala.: New Hope, 1996.
>
> Dudley, Carl S. *Next Steps in Community Ministry: Hands-On Leadership.* Bethesda: Alban Institute, 1996,

A cooperative parish of three mainline congregations in a congested urban area developed the following management design. Notice how they begin with their focus for ministry and then show how the management is integral to the work to be done. Note the interlocking frameworks of authority, with no real barriers between church and agency authority, because the task is compelling. Imagine how different the organizational structure might have been if the sponsoring churches were more hierarchical or had a theology that demanded more direct congregational control:

> *Edwin Ray United Methodist Church*
> Fountain Square C&C [Church and Community] Project will rehabilitate boarded-up houses in the neighborhood, using volunteer labor to assist home ownership for low-income families. . . . These families will work with other volunteers in the rehab process, . . . earning credits toward a down payment in exchange for hours of work.
>
> Management of the ongoing project will be at three levels. Policy decisions will be made by the Board of Governors. . . . The working committees of the board will be: executive, finances, personnel, operations, network relations, and advocacy. The next level of management is through the auspices of the [community] Investment Corporation . . . [which] has agreed to work with this project. The third level of management is on-the-job. There the person in charge will be the construction engineer, laying out the work, supervising the volunteer workers, coordinating the use of tools, and ordering supplies, etc. This person will have a working relationship with Investment Corporation, conferring with the architect assigned to the particular job, while answering to the personnel committee of the Board of Governors of the Church and Community Project.
>
> At the same level as the construction engineer and answering to the same personnel committee will be the volunteer coordinator. This person will be a Church and Community worker. Viewed as part of the pastoral team of the Fountain Square UMC assigned to the work of the Church and Community Project, this person will interrelate with life questions of volunteers and prospective homeowners.

In a more informal setting, this careful distribution of authority might be inappropriate. Notice how this rural project with two cooperating churches begins with the program and lets the organization evolve over time. Again, the planners open with a statement of purpose, but they proceed with a variety of community activities and allow the structure to bubble up from that base.

Deer Creek Presbyterian Church

Since there has been no sense of community for many years . . . the residents of the community are seen as powerless to do anything beyond individual households or land holdings to affect, nurture, change or improve community life. . . . Our first step is to develop a sense of common purpose and discover our neighbors through a series of organized activities.

A signboard will identify our community, and will tell about planned community activities. . . . The Core Committee will initially be in charge of where it will be placed and what it will say. Later the community board may expand, improve, control, etc., the signboard. . . . Out of community meetings, committees will be established to develop facilities, finances, and personnel. We envision the first step as a small place with several tables and chairs that serves drinks, donuts, and sandwiches at breakfast and lunch.

This Catholic parish reflects a radically different style of management. Although the leaders welcome input from a variety of sources, they have no question about lines of authority. Working in this setting, you would soon discover that the project staff report to the pastor, who, along with the parish council, bears the responsibility for all significant decisions:

St. Joan of Arc Catholic Church

The ministry functions will be under the direction of a full-time Director, to be hired by the Neighborhood Youth Committee. The Director will serve on the St. Joan of Arc staff and will report as designated by the pastor in day-to-day operations. The Youth Committee will induct into its membership two neighborhood youth—one a parishioner and one a non-Catholic neighbor. Matters of Policy will be decided upon by the Community Youth Committee and, if required, approved by the Parish Council.

We cannot predict by polity the management patterns that will be used by congregations in social ministry. We find independent ministries launched from Catholic churches, and Protestant ministries that report directly to the pastor. You simply "gotta know the territory," as, for example, with this Baptist congregation:

> ### *Cornell Baptist Church*
> The Steering Committee will agree upon and make recommendations to the church to be voted on during its business meeting once a month. This committee will . . . recommend a Director for hire to the church. The church will have final authority in matters of policy. . . . The Director will be accountable to the Steering Committee, with day-to-day supervision by the Pastor.

Although I have a bias for broad participation in decision making, one is unlikely to break historic congregational patterns of authority by direct confrontation. Rather, make the most of the leadership patterns you find, at least in the initial stages of program development. Leadership styles should be evaluated and adopted for the ways they contribute to achieving your ministry goals. Often leadership becomes more broadly participatory as the ministry matures, especially as volunteers influence the organization through the practice of ministry.

Develop Volunteers:
Finding and Keeping the Right People

Volunteers are the essence of church-based ministries in which members express their faith in action. They are not simply a grudging accommodation to the absence of money to pay staff. Volunteer ministries continue because members find their personal faith and church loyalty strengthened in exercising love, touching the lives of others, and being touched in return. In empowering others, we ourselves become more alive.

Your volunteers can do what professional agencies cannot do or would not attempt. Often churches can provide a functional sanctuary to many segments of a community. They may offer the only community space in a residential area and the only trusted place in an unsafe, perhaps gang-ridden, neighborhood. Churches can break through the isolation of elderly people who live scattered around the community, aggressively seek teenagers who have been abandoned by other agencies, or begin night ministries in neighborhoods where the police are the only alternative. Churches can provide a personal touch in the tutoring of children or mediate reconciliation between victims and offenders.

III.3

**RESOURCES FOR
FINDING AND SUPPORTING VOLUNTEERS**

Brackney, William H. *Christian Voluntarism: Theology and Praxis.* Manlius, N.Y.: REV/Rose Publishing, 1997.

Trumbauer, Jean Morris. *Sharing the Ministry: A Practical Guide for Transforming Volunteers into Ministers.* Minneapolis: Augsburg Fortress, 1995.

With dogged commitment and ingenious creativity, by faith your volunteers can do what social agencies cannot. But they do it as volunteers, and so they have different incentives and satisfactions, different leadership and management needs, and different standards of success. Your volunteers are generally not professional social workers, but just people who care about people. Volunteers are as much the recipients of the program as are the clients with whom they work. Your volunteers are your primary resource, the foundation of a church-based social ministry. It takes planning and imagination to make the best use of volunteers. The challenge is to link their faith motivation with your organizational program in ways that satisfy both.

In defining the tasks your committee faces, the cultivation and support of your volunteers is as important as your program and administration. One group defines the whole job with disarming simplicity:

Cornell Baptist Church
The work is one-third program hours, one-third preparation, and one-third organization of volunteers.

Volunteers bring a diversity of gifts that could not be found in any one staff professional. Typically, volunteers are interested in three broad areas: the hands-on work of ministry, support of the organization, and advocacy for changes in social structures that affect people's lives. This committee plans for all three types of involvement.

Immaculate Conception Catholic Church
Every effort will be made to involve people in the work of the Lacon Center. The Senior Citizen Survey indicates there may be room for volunteering in the areas of hospitality, transportation, yard work, light maintenance, and others. Volunteers will be involved in organizational matters as board members, keeping records, and writing the newsletter. Most of the advocacy work, including letter writing and programs, will be handled by volunteers.

This faith-based agency spends time preparing volunteer tutors; they spread them widely among many clients and help them learn together.

Covenant to Care

Volunteers also come from a variety of sources, but we try to pair up the youngster with a tutor, a one-on-one mentor. Over the next five years we hope to have several hundred people who are involved in that aspect as well.

Since every situation is different, you will need to find your own ways to involve the maximum number of interested people. Even when members are unavailable at the time a program operates, you may be able to involve them in program support and interpretation. Unfortunately, congregational size makes a difference: Larger churches usually have more access to finances, and a larger reservoir of willing volunteers. In these two examples, notice that both congregations go outside their membership to find the volunteers they need to organize their ministries.

**Figure 10.
Fund-raising and Volunteers More of a Challenge
in Smaller Congregations**

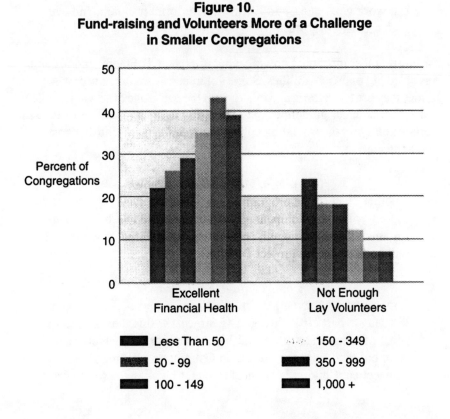

Avondale Presbyterian Church

We cannot supply many volunteers because most of our members work during the day. However, we will sponsor fund-raising dinners. We will host volunteers when they come for orientation to the program and the neighborhood. We will publicize the program by going door to door in the neighborhood, and will sponsor the open house at the beginning of the school year.

St. Michael's Catholic Church

Quite a few suburban Catholic churches help with food collection or send people in to do something with the mission work in the inner city. It works out very nicely, because it opens up their lives to new experiences, and some nice relationships have developed. Getting people from suburban churches to volunteer in this area is such a rich resource because rather than just being on the altar committee, in the city they can work with indigent elderly, they can work with teens, and . . . with the tutorial program, and even with the handicapped.

Volunteers fear most not knowing what is expected of them, and becoming involved beyond their abilities. Some volunteers want to know precisely the duties they are to perform, and others want the challenge of solving problems for which no clear guidelines exist. In either case, someone must take the responsibility for incorporating volunteers, training them, and demonstrating our appreciation:

St. Joan of Arc Catholic Church

Another facet of the program . . . is Volunteer Development and Training. The development of a volunteer cadre will be the prime responsibility of the youth committee, but training of volunteers will be done by the Project Director.

Congregation Beth Israel

So we had a Mitzvah Day in which we asked our congregants last May to participate in about 45 projects within the community. Most of them were in general kinds of programs, which ranged from building a sandbox at Camp Courant, to planting flowers at Connecticut Children's Medical Center, to working at My Sister's Place.

You can measure the success of your volunteer program because volunteers vote with their feet. The number of volunteers you can involve in every possible way is the best index of program support throughout the congregation, and volunteers are the most convincing interpreters of the ministry to the church and the larger community:

Hope Presbyterian Church

By maintaining a constant flow of information between project leaders and the congregation, we hope that members become individually excited about the mission of the project; that they will express personal concern about the issues the project addresses and share this concern with one another; that individual members become more committed to the church as [agents] to address change, and become more willing to serve.

Asylum Hill United Church of Christ

Many people join this church because they have a bent to work in Hartford. They want to do something to make a difference. In fact after we had the celebration [of volunteers on] Sunday, people kept saying, "Well, what are we doing now?" I have to find other things. . . . We are working with the neighborhood, with other churches, with community groups. . . . I have volunteers! Like, I need eight volunteers on a Saturday, and I will get 17 sign up. When I talk to people I am almost embarrassed. We have more people who want to be involved than we have involvement places.

Sometimes it's the volunteers who see the need most clearly, and adapt to a new situation with a simplicity that surprises professional agencies, as for example:

Loaves and Fishes Ministry

We have a wonderful volunteer effort of people helping us with that. People at [congregation] have been just incredible; they have a large lunch bag program that people will bring the lunch bags to church on Sunday, and they volunteer one Monday a month to bring the lunch bags here. Very big lunches—meat and cheese sandwiches, baked cookies, fruit juice, fresh fruit—a meal, definitely a full meal. Every person who comes in gets them including children; we will have 200 go out a day. They love them!

Within church programs and throughout community life, volunteers are the backbone of strength and the blood of vitality. Indeed, volunteers realize that they may be the ones who "get the most" from participating in these ministries. You can use this natural enthusiasm to close the gap between the volunteers who work in the program and the clients or recipients whom the program is designed to help. In faith, in touching another person, the healing process works both ways, and all who share in healing ministries are recipients of God's grace. Volunteers with an open and accepting attitude are the key to the next, sometimes challenging step—to include consumers as peers and sometimes the experts in the transformation of their own conditions.

Share Ministry:
Include Consumers in Basic Decisions

We minister *with* people, not *to* them. When we minister *to* people, we reduce them to objects. "They" and "we" are different. "They" are called the "clients," the "program consumers," or the "target population."

We mistakenly believe that with our resources we are powerful, and that with their needs they are weak. We are tempted to think, as the providers of ministry, that we are the decision makers, and they are the recipients.

Sharing ministry with people requires more effort. We noted above that partnerships are difficult among groups with different leadership styles, educational backgrounds, and available resources. Sharing ministry with the consumers we want to reach also crosses such social barriers as power, socioeconomic status, culture, age, and lifestyle. Bridging these differences inevitably complicates the ministry.

We make the effort to share ministry across these boundaries because we believe that all people are equal in the forgiving love of God. The purpose of our ministry is to share the empowering grace of God, not to invent new forms of dependency. Once we have experienced shared ministry, we recognize the inadequacy of more hierarchical models.

With each new generation of program participants comes the challenge to find appropriate ways for sharing ministry between those who begin by giving and others who begin by receiving.

III.4

**RESOURCES FOR
SHARING LEADERSHIP**

DePree, Max. *Leading Without Power: Finding Hope in Serving Community.* San Francisco: Jossey Bass, 1997.

Greenleaf, Robert K. Larry C. Speers, Ed. *The Power of Servant Leadership.* San Francisco: Berrett-Koehler, 1998.

At the minimum, your ministry should listen to and learn from the experiences of people who have been through your program. You can incorporate this kind of simple evaluation into almost any social ministry.

Westminster Presbyterian Church

Ongoing evaluation will be an important role of the committee to gain feedback from the clientele being served and making recommendations for changes in policy or expansion of services.

The only real experts on the needs and emotions of the people you are trying to reach are the people themselves. No matter how well your volunteers understand the conditions, empathy is not the same as having lived the problems. Some groups have drawn volunteers and trainers of volunteers from the ranks of those who have found the program helpful. Other ministries find that consumer perspectives are essential to the decision making of the board. Housing ministries, for example, have incorporated their new residents on their policy boards, and some kinds of programs for the elderly are virtually administered by the participants.

If you are concerned that the voices of one or two consumers might be stifled on a larger board, you might consider creating a separate structure to hear their views and to develop their independent leadership skills:

St. Joan of Arc Catholic Church

In an effort to encourage neighborhood youth participation in policy decisions, a Youth Council, composed of persons being served by the project [helps] the Director and the Committee benefit from the thoughts and feelings of the participants.

Empowerment is the primary focus of the next ministry, which addressed the captivity of poor families and challenged church members to break the cycle by becoming partners with the poor. Although their empowerment language reflects the influence of liberation theology, the leaders of this ministry are focused on transforming individuals and families, not changing the systems or causes of the conditions in which these people live:

Baptist Temple

Empowering people to help themselves and their community will
be our goal in Family Partners. Inviting poverty-level persons with
a desire to exit the cycle of dependency to partner with others
who care will be the direction for the project. Through a process
of shared decision making and goal setting, the project intends to
assist partner families to realize internal personal resources and
external community resources.

In whatever way works best for you, your ministry will be stronger if
you empower the recipients and affirm the equality of all participants in
building a better community, under God. The process of ministry is an
important part of its product.

GETTING THINGS DONE

When you have recognized your leadership style, defined the tasks you
need to do, found allies with a common sense of ministry, and invited
consumers to share in shaping your program, then organization is simply
your modus operandi. The best organization is the one that helps you get
things done, that accomplishes the goals of your ministry.

Focus Your Ministry

As a planning group, you are responsible to keep your ministry in focus. As noted from the FACT data (see fig. 10), congregations that are well organized and have a clarity of purpose are more likely to attract new members, and to attract participants who want to share in this ministry. Faithfulness in social ministry is its own reward, but you should not avoid the prospect of growth by lacking clarity and organization.

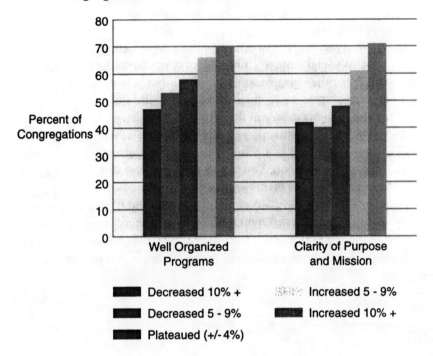

Figure 11.
Congregational Focus Relates to Membership Growth

Your appeal depends upon clear project goals and broad, effective communication. Yet even in the throes of organizing, many committees remain divided on the goals of their efforts. The most pervasive difference is between an emphasis on helping individuals and a focus on changing social systems. Different assumptions about the causes and solutions of social problems support these two perspectives; their proponents see the same world quite differently.

Some deeply committed Christians who emphasize individual responsibility for human behavior see the purpose of social ministries as caring for particular people who need help. For biblical warrants they may point to Jesus' ministry, from his first announcement in Nazareth (Luke 4:18-19) to the Son of Man judging the nations on the quality of care for "the least of these who are members of my family" (Matt. 25:31-46).

Other equally committed Christians would shift the burden of social problems away from individual responsibility, placing it at least equally on the ways in which various social, political, economic, and religious institutions have limited and frustrated "the poor and the oppressed." For biblical precedent they often reach back to the prophetic traditions and forward into early church literature in James and Revelation.

Sharp disagreements between commitments to service and to justice have put many social ministry programs on the rocks of irreconcilable differences. Yet other groups embrace these two views as ancient and honorable perspectives—two sides of the same coin, each with an imprint of its own and both necessary in the fullness of ministry.

As the group most directly responsible for the development of your ministry, your committee is a primary source for interpreting the purpose and meaning of the program. You can exacerbate these differences, or you can find a yoke to harness them together for the sake of a stronger program and for people from the larger community who would like to support your ministry—sometimes for different reasons. Most congregations begin with service and then move toward justice as the "client" becomes a friend, and together they identify the entrenched, external forces that perpetuate their problems.

SERVICE MINISTRIES: ACTING WITH CHRISTIAN COMPASSION

Initially, ministries of service to individuals may seem most natural to your church planning committee. These caring activities reflect the personal quality of relationships among the members of most congregations. Even large churches see themselves as caring communities, especially when individuals are infirm or troubled. Both our faith and our culture highly value this personal, individual care. For some churches this compassion is embedded in their habits and carried in their reputation throughout the community.

Reflecting this emphasis on each individual, your church may approach social ministry as a natural expression of faith in response to human need. In describing your ministry this way, you can mobilize some of the strongest Christian values prized by your church members. In narrative and in pictures, most church literature interpreting social ministry depicts the compassion of our ministries in response to the needs of particular persons—the vulnerable child, the broken family, the isolated elderly adult.

Caring runs a risk, however, of perpetuating inequality and dependency. Your committee will need to push the congregation to understand social ministry as something more than providing help for less fortunate people. Reflecting faith communities that witness to God's transforming power, church social ministries should encourage and empower individuals to grow into the fullness of their God-given possibilities. Ministries to individual needs may at one time be as supportive as a mother's love, yet may later become as inhibiting as a parent who hangs on to children long after they are grown.

Your committee can shape a ministry of service that will care for people when they need help and will also empower people to faith and personal fulfillment. You can help members of the congregation to grow by including them in events that help both "server and servee" to mature together. For those without direct contact with your program, you can have an impact on the rest of their lives by the way you help them to appreciate what their church is doing in ministry, and to share in it, even from a distance.

Youth are a primary concern for many social ministries, for they represent the next generation, the future of the church and the community:

St. Joan of Arc Catholic Church

As our project begins, we will target the young people of our neighborhood. We will address their needs in the particulars of Education and Life-Skills; Health, Recreation and Faith Development, Employment and Economic Betterment. Our program will consist of Formal Tutoring, Counseling, Advocacy Referrals, and Organized Sports.

Notice how this ministry begins with a focus on the needs of the elderly but moves toward strengthening whole families:

Community United Church of Christ

Daybreak Inc. will provide an adult day health care service for the community. The project will offer older adults the opportunity to maintain or improve their level of functioning, enabling them to remain in a private home setting for as long as possible. . . . In addition, the project will improve the relationships among family members coping with the stress of care giving.

Some programs combine the needs of one group with the skills of another. In this project the teenagers learn home repair and maintenance while the elderly have their homes repaired. The combined effect will change the community attitude and climate.

Washburn Christian Church

We want to work together to train people who are unskilled, including high school students, to learn maintenance and repair through restoring property in need of improvement in our communities. We will be doing one property at a time, when needed, as supervising personnel is available. Our goal is to strengthen community pride and renew hope for the future.

You can ground your service ministry in congregational and community commitments to respond to people who need help. If helping the needy is your only motive, however, you may create new dependencies. By seeking ways of empowering others, you strengthen those who are served and those who provide the service. Both are more fully human—physically, mentally, and spiritually—in the equality of the exchange.

JUSTICE MINISTRIES: CHALLENGING DYSFUNCTIONAL SYSTEMS

With more experience in service ministries, or a different emphasis in community analysis, congregations may shift to advocate changing the external forces that are perpetuating their community problems. Such ministries of justice begin with a different assumption.

Although they may be equally concerned with individual growth, they place a far greater emphasis on the havoc caused by ineffective and destructive systems. They insist that social evils will not changed until concerned citizens change such dysfunctional structures as the educational institutions that leave students illiterate, employment programs that ignore the displaced worker, government housing agencies that cannot shelter those who need it most, police who break

---

III.5
RESOURCES FOR
DIFFERING VIEWS FOR SOCIAL MINISTRY

Jacobsen, Dennis A. *Doing Justice: Congregations and Community Organizing.* Minneapolis: Fortress, 2001.

Keller, Timothy, *Ministries of Mercy: The Call of the Jericho Road.* Phillipsburg, N.J.: P&R Publisher, 1997.

Streeter, Ryan. *Transforming Charity: Toward a Results-Oriented Social Sector.* Indianapolis: Hudson Institute, 2001.

the law more than enforce it, and courts that neither satisfy the victims nor reclaim the criminals.

Justice ministries point the finger of responsibility toward the institutions that not only fail in their tasks but leave people scared and unable to find a foothold in society. They want to confront the sources of the problems rather than blame the victims of these failing institutions. Justice ministries require special training to empower volunteers with facts about conditions and their causes, and with a time for psychic adjustment from one mindset to another.

This emphasis on justice seems foreign to church members whose primary focus is on serving people in need. Justice ministries challenge inadequate systems, while service ministries help needy people. Justice ministries use collective, sometimes confrontational tactics to change institutions, while service ministries use personal relationships to strengthen individuals and families. Justice efforts advocate changes in policies and programs, while service seeks support for individuals in transition. Combining compassion and justice often begins when leaders make clear that justice is as important as compassion, as these leaders suggest:

Catholic Officer of Urban Affairs
Advocacy. The word "advocacy" scares a lot of [church people]. There are very simple things they can do which would be considered advocacy, including paying a great deal of attention to how they vote and what is going on in the legislature, and holding their legislators responsible for some of their decisions they are about to make.

Bethel AME Church
I am going to move on their behalf, to be a voice for the voiceless and a champion for the oppressed. I preach a lot in the church that, "If it ain't about justice, it ain't about Jesus."

The sharp lines of justice seem to blur in the pragmatic challenge of doing ministry. Notice how easily this youth program builds a bridge from advocacy for the needs of individual students to advocacy for changes in the educational system.

Good News Community Church

GNC's commitment to social justice expresses itself through advocacy with parents, teachers, employers, and legislators. The GNC director will stay in direct communication with both parents and employers as a teen advocate, and . . . the local high school to determine the progress of GNC's teenagers and to intervene as necessary. This may lead to intervention with the school board on policy matters or other intervention at the local level.

The leaders of this elderly care program are much more aware of the distinction between service and justice and of a progression from one to the other. They build on a network of service agencies and the trust of clients as a foundation for pressing for legislative changes regarding Alzheimer's disease.

Community United Church of Christ

Advocacy is defined as pleading another person's cause and is also understood as "treating the disease, not the symptoms." One of the goals of adult day care is to provide services to both the participants and caregiver families, facilitating integration into the community's health and social network. As we gain experience and trust of clients and caregivers we will be constantly alert for other areas where we may become effective advocates. A case in point may be raising public consciousness on the need for legislation to identify Alzheimer's and related disorders as health conditions qualifying for Medicare and insurance coverage.

This group in a rural town has been hit by a recession of the farm economy and a cutback in regional industrial employment. Group members are seeking ways to deal with their triple problems of declining income, lost employment, and deteriorating housing. But, like most effective justice ministries, they do not seek to act alone. Rather, they have formed a council or coalition to translate the relational issues of service ministries into challenges for systemic change.

Washburn Christian Church

We will continue to study the root cause of poverty, unemployment, and poor housing. We feel we must take social action plus service to minister properly to the poor. . . . [We have] a community council with a legislative agenda for support of the jobless, including legislation concerning plant closings and layoffs, and mortgage foreclosures.

An urban housing ministry understands its work as far more than construction and renovation. The community has not been transformed until the residents have a say in the policies that shape the future of the area. In this situation the project leaders recognize the oppression of intangible economic and political forces, but they lift up the Christian vision of a fully integrated neighborhood that looks beyond the necessities and welcomes the gifts each person brings. In their project goals they have comfortably yoked housing for individual families with transformation of the community.

Edwin Ray United Methodist Church
One of the continuing responsibilities of the core committee is advocacy for [with] the poor. . . . To stand with them, to be present to their struggles, to interpret meaningfully the work of the project . . . are responsibilities of the core committee. . . . It must work with constancy to hold up the vision of an economically (as well as in other ways) integrated neighborhood, which honors the right to the necessities of life for everyone, and which appreciates that all people have their gifts to offer to the community if their voices are heard and their confidence empowered. Linked with this is discerning what blocks the informant from available resources.
  Also, the core committee will be supportive of these families as they organize to change city policies, patterns and decisions of banks and other institutions that function to seriously limit options which should rightfully be theirs if they are to function responsibly.

Often the transition from compassion to justice is simply taking a risk, instead of taking things for granted, as this church leader laments.

Christian Conference of Connecticut
I would like to see us take some risks. . . . I think what we are doing is wonderful, but the issues of the city are extremely daunting, and we need to take some risks and try to advocate for change.

Fit Your Identity

Your project interpretation must clarify purpose and mobilize resources. The energy of your project will depend upon volunteers, fund raising, and staff. In organizing for your ministry, you will need to shape numerous elements to fit your identity, including managerial style, group expectations, partner development, and the empowerment of people with whom you are working. The whole task is dynamic: all the parts are interdependent, and no part is so fixed in place that it no longer needs your attention. Organization just keeps on happening.

In building your organization, your goal is not a blueprint or a managerial chart. Rather, you should shape an organization that fits your situation, finds fresh energy in the congregation's faith, and, above all, is appropriate to get the job done.

Organizing for Social Ministry

Step 1: Build Organization (pp. 111-114)

We have written an initial ministry proposal and plan.
Date: _____ *Assigned to:*_____

We have identified and discussed the organizational plan or decision-making process of our congregation.
Date: _____ *Assigned to:*_____

We have designed and agree on an initial organizational structure for our community ministry, which will grow with our ministry.
Date: _____ *Assigned to:*_____

Step 2: Develop Volunteers (pp. 115-120)

We appreciate what motivates volunteers and what scares them.
Date: _____ *Assigned to:*_____

We have designed a plan to recruit, train, and support volunteers for our community ministry.
Date: _____ *Assigned to:* _____

Step 3: Share Ministry (pp. 121-123)

We plan to include recipients of our ministry in initial evaluations..
Date: _____ *Assigned to:* _____

We have plans to include ministry recipients in the ministry itself.
Date: _____ *Assigned to:* _____

Step 4: Focus Your Ministry (pp. 124-132)
We have essential clarity of purpose for the proposed ministry.
Date: _____ *Assigned to:* _____

We are combining compassion and justice in the ways that faithfully reflect the basic needs of our community.
Date: _____ *Assigned to:* _____

Big Steps toward Social Ministry

PART IV

Big Steps toward Social Ministry

M ost congregations care about helping people, beginning with basics in emergencies and expanding in a variety of directions. The national crisis of September 11, 2001, taught us that we are vulnerable, like other nations. The experience has affected our spiritual sensibilities in many ways as well. As a nation we rediscovered the precious qualities of personal relationships, the value of a caring community, and the capacity to feel the pain of people we do not know personally—not only as values to be remembered, but as commitments to be practiced.

But habits change slowly, even in cataclysmic times. The sudden surge in overt religious participation (attending worship, reading Scripture) returned to normal in most places beyond sight of Ground Zero. "The evidence from churches and synagogues, combined with several polls, now indicates that for most people the spiritual storm has passed, except perhaps in New York, where the pain of the attack is most intense."[1] In this sense 9/11 lingers in consciousness that may slowly be translated into action.

Figure 12.
Community Ministries of Crisis, Nurture, and Intervention

List of Community Outreach Ministries............................. YES%

CRISIS MINISTRIES FOR EMERGENCY HELP
Cash assistance to families or individuals............................ 88%
Food pantry or soup kitchen... 85%
Clothing closet/thrift shop... 60%
Crisis hotline or counseling.. 46%
Hospital or nursing home... 45%
Emergency or affordable housing....................................... 38%

NURTURING PROGRAMS FOR EDUCATION, HEALTH, AND QUALITY OF LIFE
Senior citizen programs.. 45%
Day care, etc. for children... 36%
Tutoring or literacy.. 32%
Health programs or clinics.. 32%
Employment programs... 21%
Migrant/immigrant... 14%

INTERVENTION INITIATIVES FOR PERSONAL OR COMMUNITY CHANGE
Prison or jail ministry... 38%
Substance abuse... 33%
Advocate justice issues.. 29%
Voter education.. 29%

Ministries differ in goals, conditions, and intensity of commitments. Looking again at the reports from congregations in the FACT study, we can distinguish three kinds of social ministry—crisis ministries in response to emergencies, nurture ministries in long-term care, and transformation ministries that seek to intervene and change individuals or communities (see fig. 12). Note that far more congregations are involved in responding to emergencies among their members and in the lives of people in their own communities. In a crisis, congregations provide important but temporary relief. In nurturing ministries, congregations support programs for education, health, and social life. Typically these programs are done with other church and agency partners, organized by professionals, and supported by volunteers. Intervention ministries are less likely to be housed and organized by single congregations, since they require more professional leaders who work with fewer and more specialized volunteers. Transformation ministries are frequently a local expression of a larger program in which the congregation shares in a movement or cause greater than itself.

When we see that almost nine out of ten faith communities of all sorts are engaged in crisis care, the data in figure 12 explain why religious steeples and domes are seen as the ultimate safety net for the lives of so many people across the country. The chart gives credibility to the responses of most clergy who, when asked about social ministries, describe the crises they see daily in their own communities. Congregations describe different strategies but similar goals.

St. Michael's Catholic Church
So often people will stop at the rectory and ask for assistance with their fuel bill or medications; that seems to be the two major issues.

Mount Olive Baptist Church
Anybody who comes in and says they are hungry, we don't give cash money out to nobody. If they say they want food, clothing, or some kind of furniture, we won't give you the money for it; we will get it for you. That's what we do.

Most caring ministries are sustained, like these, in efforts to make the most of meager resources. From the constant flow of need and response, St. Peter's Church has a rhythm of seasons and locations.

St. Peter's Catholic Church
Whatever comes in usually goes right out. Whatever doesn't go right out gets picked over, and we usually send it to the Third World. The things are usually in good shape and winter things don't move in the summer, but they will do well in the Andes. So there is a constant recycling going on into and from the parish.

Volunteer-based ministries in response to crisis conditions can relieve the symptoms but have little energy remaining to change the causes. The chart makes very clear that members want to be helpful, and, as volunteer-based groups, they are making heroic contributions. In the changing landscape of the 21st century, more need is recognized, more resources are offered, and more risk is assumed by congregations that respond.

EXPLORING DECISIONS FOR EXPANDING YOUR MINISTRY

These are big steps reflecting a quantum leap, a change of scope and scale in community ministry. By reporting the options, we are not urging congregations to move up a league into this new field of play. In fact, we strongly advocate that individual congregations of any size smaller than the largest churches, probably should not expand their ministries without professional staff and in-place agreements for program oversight. Congregations that care about community conditions are faced with four significant choices. In these broad areas, decisions will not be made once and forever, but these continue to haunt the edges of your work, options that you might take at any time. In this landscape of crying need, scarce but creative resources, and innovative opportunities, you will be making these decisions more than once, even when the choice is negative.

BIG STEP 1. ESTABLISH YOUR MINISTRY NICHE

As government offers "charitable choice" or other funding, faith-based ministries must be intentional to develop a niche among a wide array of services.

BIG STEP 2. EMPLOY STAFF AND RAISE MONEY

Larger ministries need staff to extend, not replace, the work of volunteers, and staff increases costs exponentially.

BIG STEP 3. DEVELOP PARTNERS AND MEDIATORS

Institutional networks are essential both to strengthen and to protect local ministries.

BIG STEP 4. ENHANCE SPIRITUAL EXPERIENCES

Social ministries can bring a uniquely transforming power to all who participate in these communities of the Spirit.

Establish Your Ministry Niche

As congregations face the spiritual and physical needs of people in their communities (or larger region) they might explore the option to expand their ministries to reach more people, and reach them more effectively. As these ministries touch the lives of individuals, families, and community groups, they are naturally incorporated into the fabric of community care—as churches want to help, others begin to expect it of them.

With congregations showing such a high level of involvement, especially in crisis ministries, little wonder that government agencies concerned about social welfare would be interested in sharing the load. Responsible state agencies are particularly attracted to work with congregations that are located in areas of greatest need, because they have members, contacts, and creditability in these communities of need. Since these indigenous assets of space and trust make congregations especially appealing, outside agencies may push congregations to move from small and manageable programs like soup kitchens and clothing pantries to more extended and complex ministries, such as day care, a health clinic, drug rehab, or job training.

For many years in cities throughout the country, local schools, police, and welfare departments have worked in and through particular congregations to offer extended and highly professional social ministries in the community. In addition, nationally recognized religious agencies like the Salvation Army, Catholic Charities, Lutheran Family Services, and the Jewish Federation have developed an enviable track record of contract-for-services to families and individuals in need. For a generation, government agencies have provided oversight and assistance to faith-based educational and health programs in every kind of community, especially in the pressured areas of center cities (see fig. 13). Legally these programs that worked with "tax dollars" have been prohibited from exposing clients to sectarian religious symbols, literature, or activity. Faith-based programs provided "services," as suggested by this faith-based program staff person in describing his contractual relationship with *government agencies*:

Figure 13.
Ministries with Government Oversight:
Day Care and Health Programs

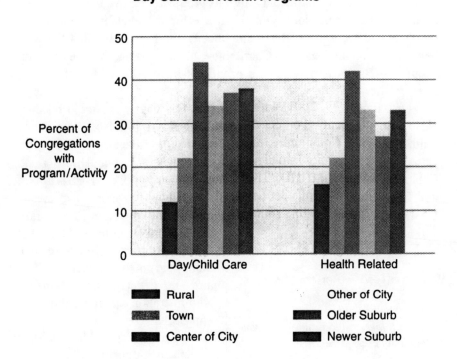

Glory Chapel International Cathedral/Youth Challenge
Interfacing with the state, sometimes you are dealing with agencies that might not feel comfortable with the spiritual component. But they don't have a problem because the roof is provided, the shelter, all the support services, heat in the winter, hot water, three meals a day for all the residents, transportation to and from clinic and legal appointments.

In the context of that extended and pervasive working relationship, federal welfare reform legislation of 1996 included the so called "Charitable

Choice" provision, requiring that religious organizations be permitted to receive funding "on the same basis" as any other nongovernmental provider. Specifically the law would allow "charitable, religious or private organizations" to apply for and receive competitive grants for services rendered. The new law, in effect, "baptized" existing practice, with this exception: To receive federal welfare funds, states would no longer be expected to require contractual religious groups to remove their art, icons, Scripture, or other religious symbols. In an effort to "level the playing field" (as President George W. Bush announced), the law dismantled the wall between church and state. In Charitable-Choice funding, the line between secular services and religious practices became a wide margin of interpretation.

On January 29, 2001, within his first few days in office, President Bush signed executive orders that established a White House Office of Faith-Based and Community Initiatives and supportive Centers for Faith-Based and Community Initiatives in five agencies—Justice, Housing and Urban Development (HUD), Health and Human Services (HHS), Labor, and Education. With this act he greatly expanded the scope of previous Charitable-Choice funding sources beyond the initial welfare, Temporary Aid to Needy Families (TANF), and related programs. But more than money, he put the force of his office and the prestige of his infant administration squarely behind this approach.

In a personal appeal to a national interfaith gathering of religious leaders at the time of proposing this new initiative, President Bush made his priorities clear:

Everyone in this room knows there are still deep needs and real suffering in the shadow of America's affluence—problems like addiction, abandonment, and gang violence, domestic

---

IV.1
RESOURCES FOR FAITH-BASED MINISTRIES

Jeavons, Thomas. *When the Bottom Line Is Faithfulness*. Bloomington: Indiana University Press, 1993.

Sherman, Amy L. *Restorer of Hope: Reaching the Poor in Your Community with Church-based Ministries That Work*. Wheaton, Ill.: Crossways Books, 1997.

Sider, Ronald J., Philip N. Olson, and Heidi Rolland Unruh. *Churches That Make a Difference: Reaching Your Community with Good News and Good Works.* Grand Rapids: Baker Boooks, 2001.

violence, mental illness and homelessness. We are called by conscience to respond. . . . It is one of the great goals of my administration to invigorate the spirit of involvement and citizenship. We will encourage faith-based and community programs without changing their mission. We will help all in their work to change hearts while keeping a commitment to pluralism. . . .

Government will never be replaced by charities and community groups. Yet when we see social needs in America, my administration will look first to faith-based programs and community groups, which have proven their power to save and change lives. . . . We will make sure that help goes to large organizations and to small ones as well. We also value neighborhood healers, who have only the scars and testimony of their own experience.

As information concerning the prospect of Charitable Choice funding filtered through the media and layers of social service bureaucracy, the responses we heard in congregations and agencies could be broadly clustered into two concerns—the first about religious groups receiving government money, and the second about the process by which those funds might be distributed.

RESPONSES TO CHARITABLE CHOICE

Concerning the potential for new funding, the range of responses in Hartford, Connecticut, congregations would seem to reflect the nation in microcosm. Some leaders are convinced that any compromise in the separation of church and state will undermine foundational beliefs:

Congregation Beth Israel
Jews feel very, very strongly about the separation between church and state. So we are not supporters of that notion of public funding through religious based organizations for social service, because there will always be some kind of content related to it.

Glory Chapel International Cathedral/Youth Challenge
Our Board feels so strongly that they did not want to compromise what they knew to be the "active ingredient," that is, faith.

The opposite view was expressed from faith-based programs whose leaders feel the need to expand their resources to meet pressing human needs, while believing that they are well protected against secular intrusion into their beliefs.

St. Michael's Catholic Church

Would we try to get federal monies? I don't think we would have any scruples if we saw a need that was not being met and our parish could do that for the neighborhood. It certainly is one of our goals to be responsive to the needs of the community.

Covenant to Care

Would we have a problem in applying for government grants? Oh no! We would certainly do it if it looked like something that fit into our mission and was available to us. And we have had DCF funding since the second year we were around. . . . DCF requires that we fund a minimum of 25 percent of our budget, so we have to find it somewhere. If we could find it through federal funds, that would be dynamite.

Rather than a clear separation between faith-based and secular agencies, we discovered that existing social ministries were embedded in a network of private and public funding that made ministry possible. Some maintained the myth of autonomy by honestly reporting their condition, but with a catch. Thus:

Loaves and Fishes, Inc.

We are completely privately funded. We do not have a cent of city, state, or federal money. Really, that is a wonderful comment on this community. It really truly is. Our funding breaks down almost exactly one-third, one-third, one-third: one-third religious organizations (churches and synagogues), one-third foundations and corporations, and one-third in small gifts.

The director is accurate and honest, but at the same time, most staff in the program were paid through a job-training program of federal funding, and the food supply had a federally funded subsidy. No government money was received, but the feeding program could not operate without a wide variety of appropriate but completely unseen government financial support.

Perhaps this leader captures the ambiguity that many feel about
government funding being used to support faith-based community ministries:

St. Peter's Catholic Church
In our parish there is really a desire for separation of church and
state. It is still very strong. But people get around it in other ways.

Beyond program concerns, the process of Charitable Choice worried
even more leaders of social ministries. They greeted the offer with deep
reservations about the political motives in Washington, and in general:

Bethel AME Church
With almost 30 years of ministry now, I confess to you that I am
very cynical about the political process. . . .

HART—Hartford Areas Rally Together
Part of the frustration is that we know there are a lot of state
dollars, for instance, that are there to be used, and just don't get
used for this. Forty million dollars' worth of State TANF money
that could have been used for providing day care and training—
and it just disappeared! It got absorbed into the state budget and
was reallocated.

St. John's Episcopal Church
Sounds like welfare legislation is nothing more than rhetoric—a
way for the federal government to shirk its responsibility for the
welfare of society's needy.

Some warned about "smoke and mirrors" on both sides, and worried if
congregations were prepared for the problems they would inherit.

Capital Region Conference of Churches
So. . . the real question of Charitable Choice is, I think, two-sided:
One side is a smokescreen—it pretends that there are alternatives
to governments support for welfare, when there really are not—
and the second is that the churches are conned into accepting
responsibility so that the feds and the state can dump on the
churches and say, "Now it is your problem, not ours."

Virtually universal were concerns about program and fiscal management that seemed implied by granting Charitable Choice. These are typical comments:

Divine Light Baptist Church

The red tape—they give you something, and then they put so many restrictions on it, you can't use it. . . . Because you see, when the government gives you a dollar, they put a thousand restrictions on it. They give it to you to do this, but then they turn around and say you can't do it. So we need funds to do what we can do, what we have been designed to do—and that is, to get a child, bring him or her in, and begin with our program of training and discipline. Sometimes that does not meet with the government's standards. . . . I used to be a politician one time . . . and I figured out that pastors ain't got no business being politicians.

One Chane, Inc.

Our experiences with the city have been horrible! One grant [we] have had with the city has been frozen for two years because of political problems.

Asylum Hill Congregational Church

Maybe it is because I made that choice when I took the job, knowing that politics in Hartford is a combat sport.

Churches elsewhere that have assumed commitments to develop faith-based ministries have often taken on far more than their capacity to produce, and they find themselves unable to fulfill their contractual agreements. One stark example, cited by Robert Wineburg, a UNC-Greensboro professor of social work, occurred in North Carolina:

The Department of Social Services put a $10,000 contract on the table for . . . a new faith-based nonprofit. . . . I asked the director to look carefully at items A-H. . . . the true cost [of developing the administrative infrastructure to implement the program according to state specifications] came to $75,000.[2]

In short, it's the process, not the program, that makes these congregations hesitate at the level of Charitable Choice-funded ministries.

Local congregations, even with extensive experience in crisis ministries, are ill equipped and vulnerable when they face the quantum leap required to enter and fulfill long-term, complex contracts for ministry services. Charitable Choice funds are available because they are needed, and faith-based ministries have a history of positive service in difficult communities. But even with the most loyal volunteers, solo churches cannot be expected to play on such a large and undefined arena. The first Big Step is just the beginning, and the others are essential for survival. At this point you need staff and money, you need partners and mediators, you need clarity of faith and depth of purpose—the next Big Steps to community ministry.

Employ Staff and Raise Money

Ministries that begin with the energy of volunteers often expand to stretch beyond the capacities of unpaid staff to get it all done, and do it all again and again. Even when they are not greatly expanding or taking on new responsibilities, faith-based ministries often need part-time staff (or part of the time of staff with other assignments) to give continuity to the program and save the efforts of volunteers for direct contact experiences. Sometimes these programs need continuity of information, or coordination of volunteers, or simple consistency in their program and practices.

The transition from a volunteer program to paid staff, even part time, is significant. Some ministries begin with one or more people who were previously volunteers. Other programs take the plunge with a single, full-time employee who provides anything from simple administration to highly trained professional leadership. It is a big step that can resolve many nagging organizational problems and significantly stabilize your social ministry.

But this step is the most unpredictable element in building a ministry program. Selecting and supervising staff can be an Achilles' heel even for well-organized, fully supported programs. Numerous materials are available to explain the financial and personnel-management aspects of this move. From

---

IV.2

RESOURCES FOR ENLARGING MINISTRIES

Perkins, John. *Restoring At-Risk Communities*. Grand Rapids: Baker Books, 1995.

Queen, Edward L. II, ed. *Serving Those in Need: A Handbook for Managing Faith-Based Human Services Organizations*. San Francisco: Jossey-Bass, 2000.

Skjegstad, Joy. *Starting a Non-Profit at Your Church*. Bethesda: Alban Institute, 2002.

our experience I will highlight the relatively unique challenge when a community ministry moves to integrate paid staff into a previously all volunteer-based program.

INCORPORATING PROFESSIONALS WITH VOLUNTEERS

Although professional leadership may be needed and welcome, it can be awkward to bring a paid staff member into a program organized and served by volunteers. Even when job definitions, expectations, and accountabilities are clearly stated, the lines between volunteers and paid staff are never sufficiently precise to cover every circumstance. Consider the dilemma if some volunteers relax their efforts because the staff is "paid to do the job," while others feel offended that the same staff person has "taken over." Unfortunately, under these pressures, volunteers and staff can become suspicious of each other's motives.

Further, in a new church-based ministry, the staff is often less experienced and underpaid, compared with employees of more established, professional agencies. Providing adequate compensation seems to be a relentless problem. Typically, board leaders and even the pastor are equally inexperienced in supervising staff. In addition, social ministries that are responsive to community needs are often growing and changing. Particularly in newly organized ministries, initial job descriptions rapidly become outdated and need to be changed. Both volunteers and staff need to amend their ways of thinking and interpret agreements flexibly—sometimes an invitation to conflict. You will need a sustaining faith, a trust in people, and a strong dose of good humor to incorporate staff into your voluntary program.

Some faith-based programs begin with part-time staff. Notice the qualifications for the part-time employees discussed below. They are expected to have values similar to those of the volunteers, but knowledge and cultural affinity that go beyond the skills and sensitivities of the current church members:

Avondale Presbyterian Church
We feel that in order to run a strong program we will need to hire three people on a part-time basis: a director who will be in charge of planning the program and running it, and two assistants. We do not feel that these paid staff must have specific academic

qualifications. We are looking for men and women who love children and enjoy working with them. We would prefer people from the general area, people who know city life and the dynamics of Chicago neighborhoods. Because of the high number of Hispanics in the neighborhood, we plan to hire one bilingual worker so communication with Hispanic parents can be facilitated.

Whatever the qualifications, you will need to be especially clear about the responsibilities and accountability of staff, while not being so detailed that the job description inhibits personal initiative or prohibits growth with the maturing of the ministry:

Cornell Baptist Church

A paid director will direct and manage the project, plan the day-to-day program, organize and manage volunteers, supervise other paid staff, record attendance and effectiveness measures, and be responsible for publicity. The director will be a member of the Advisory Board and an ex-officio, nonvoting member of the steering committee. As such, the director may make suggestions to the steering committee on matters of policy. The Director will be accountable to the steering committee, with day-to-day supervision by the pastor.

Some committees expect growth and transition. Although change may not occur in the anticipated way, such language invites similar flexibility in other aspects of the program:

Edwin Ray United Methodist Church

The positions of construction engineer and volunteer coordinator will be needed long range. The bookkeeper-financial officer is expected to go from being an unpaid volunteer to one with a stipend through a retired volunteers program.

For the protection of both the board and the employee, include a procedure for employee review, affirmation, and redirections:

First Meridian Heights Presbyterian Church

[The employee] will have an opportunity for quarterly formal interchange regarding job satisfaction and performance.

Disagreements will be brought to the attention of the board of managers for a final resolution.

The right staff person can transform every aspect of the program, but perhaps best of all he or she can bring new levels of confidence and satisfaction to everyone who participates. At the same time this is a quantum leap for the internal dynamics of your ministry, and for the financial obligation of your lay leaders.

FUND RAISING: CONQUERING YOUR RELUCTANCE

Additional funding is not a separate step, but an essential part of adding paid staff to your ministry program. In fact, many programs know that they need employed help but cannot imagine raising the money to support such a leap in financial responsibilities.

Money problems are emotional barriers to the development of many social ministries. Churches have budgeted for their own needs, including established benevolences. They have a pattern of giving that they understand and anticipate continuing, and they may find it hard to imagine supporting a new social ministry within their current financial situation. After years of effort, they feel that the church income is fixed and predictable. Or, worse, they often feel that it is fragile and perhaps declining. They often cannot see the needs for community ministry simply because they cannot imagine that they have the resources to support such a program, particularly with paid staff.

The challenge of fund raising is to find new sources of revenue to support the social ministry without undermining the current budget for all the other commitments of the congregation. First, leaders must expand their concept of stewardship.

In many congregations stewardship is narrowly focused on fund raising from members to support the internal functions of worship, education, and the fellowship life of the church. But when you expand stewardship to embrace the use of all God's gifts to support and strengthen all God's people, then you have a rationale that offers access to raise money from a much larger array of community resources.

That is, when you understand your social ministry as God's activity that makes a difference in the world beyond your congregation—touching individuals and transforming communities—then your committee can effectively solicit businesses and individuals outside the church membership. When the ministry is for the community beyond the congregation, you can ask corporations, foundations, and even agencies of government to join in your outreach. If your sense of stewardship includes caring for the community through and beyond the church membership, you can open a whole range of new financial resources not otherwise available to self-contained congregational programs.

IV.3

**RESOURCES FOR
FUND-RAISING TRENDS AND CHOICES**

Hoge, Dean R., et al. *Money Matters: Personal Giving in American Churches.* Louisville: Westminster John Knox, 1996.

_____. *Plain Talk about Churches and Money.* Bethesda: Alban Institute, 1997.

Mead, Loren. *Financial Meltdown in the Mainline?* Bethesda: Alban Institute, 1998.

Rosso, Henry A., and Associates. *Achieving Excellence in Fund Raising: A Comprehensive Guide to Principles, Strategies and Methods.* San Francisco: Jossey-Bass, 1991.

Wuthnow, Robert. *The Crisis in the Churches: Spiritual Malaise, Fiscal Woe.* Oxford, England: Oxford University Press, 1997.

The financial support required depends on your goals and your plans to achieve them. Personnel is the most significant cost variable in virtually every program, and faith-based programs are often attractive because the number of volunteers would appear to reduce staff costs. Tutoring and youth sports programs, for example, can be operated with minimal budgets, except for the cost of staff who coordinate and give continuity to the program. Pantries and meal programs generally need many volunteers and a few paid regulars. Counseling and day-care programs typically require more professionals, and housing programs usually demand substantial financing. But when matched with comparable professional agencies, faith-based programs are able to provide more services at lower cost through the use of volunteers, low overhead, and in-kind contributions.

While you may not need the large budget of a professional agency, you will need more money than can be secured from your bake sales and Sabbath offerings. In most cases the money can be found "through prayer and fasting"—which might be translated "through imagination and hard work."

Financial support is so significant that you should confront the problem directly with a committee that makes fund raising its primary task:

First Meridian Heights Presbyterian Church
A volunteer chairperson and subcommittee from the churches
and the community . . . have no other task for the project but to
seek out funds.

Since 90 percent of charitable giving comes from individuals, you should
aggressively tell your story to selected people throughout your community.
When convinced of your cause, sometimes they can help directly, but often
they have contacts and creative suggestions. Smaller towns may have fewer
resources, but the people who live there have more access to each other,
as seen in the planning of this small-town housing project to attract the
attention of neighbors:

Washburn Christian Church
We will continue to request donations from individuals within our
community. We will let them know about the tax credits to
individuals and businesses [that] invest in development that provides
low and moderate income housing. . . . [We will] have a work-a-
thon where volunteers work on a project (elderly persons' home
needing a new roof). The volunteers get other people to sponsor
them. . . . We will paint a giant thermometer and put it in a
prominent place in town with our goal at the top. As we advertise
our needs and educate the community, we will let all know where
we stand in donations. . . . We will develop a mailing list of donors.
They will be kept informed about how our project is proceeding,
when unexpected needs arise, and successes by mail. We will
express thanks as we meet our goals.

Your denominational body may have sources of funding that you should
explore, both through the formal agencies of the church and in the informal
networks among pastors or churches:

Edwin Ray United Methodist Church
Funding will come from grants, from suburban churches, Metro
Ministries, District, Conference, and National Division Mission
sources of the United Methodist Church.

Small-town neighbors and denominational ties reflect the importance
of personal connections in fund raising: people give to other people they
know and trust, in small towns and big cities alike.

Although sometimes local and well-known sources are sufficient, you will need a more diversified approach to support your ministry. Notice how this committee begins with the sources that are nearest and most involved in the ministry, and then moves out to seek funding from other agencies that share their concern. Although they are church-based, they recognize possible sources that other churches often ignore:

Irvington United Methodist Church

Initially, we expect the fund-raising program to cover the following sources: (1) The contract and partnering organizations will be contacted to determine the amount of financial support available from each. (2) A prospective donor list will be developed of individuals in the community who might be able and willing to contribute financially to the project. (3) A listing will be developed of all corporations which have some relationship to the community or the project and contact will be made to determine the proper approach to request corporate financial support. (4) From resource listing of foundations, contact will be made to determine procedures for developing the opportunities for financial support and preparation of grant proposals. (5) Public sector government agencies will be contacted to determine any programs which might provide financial support for the project. (6) When appropriate, user fees based on a sliding scale will be established.

Mainline churches that limit their income to "tithes and offerings" (or pledges and bequests) could take a lesson from Roman Catholic and black Churches in impacted urban areas that scramble to assemble money from countless sources simply to respond to the needs on their doorstep.

Phillips Metropolitan CME Church

We have a neighborhood networks technology center for the community. Phillips and several Hartford congregations have partnered with the Department of Children and Families in the Esther Project, which supports foster and adoptive families. Phillips, First Cathedral, the Urban League, and the Department of Mental Health and Addiction Services are in collaboration to provide support to children whose parents have substance abuse issues. Our partnership with the Hartford Public Schools will bring a full-service Adult Education Center to our neighborhood. We are in collaboration with the City of Hartford and the Hartford Economic Development Commission to strengthen our efforts to revitalize blighted areas along Main Street. Through Phillip's nonprofit corporation's partnership with the Sheldon Oak Central Inc., we received a HUD 202 grant to construct 40 units of senior housing. We have food banks, an after school tutoring program, . . . [list of 50-some programs].

One of the unanticipated benefits of the national discussion on Charitable Choice is the way it has stimulated the dreams of many congregational leaders about what more they might do with expanded resources. New combinations of congregations are gathering to explore options, and existing ministry leaders are imagining an expansion. Charitable Choice caused a new recognition of the many sources of income necessary to keep these ministries going. A strongly evangelical leader makes this point clear:

Glory Chapel International Cathedral/Youth Challenge
We have a wide variety of people who support us. Specific congregations. Congregational churches, Episcopal churches, Lutheran churches, Assembly of God churches. . . . I think that people recognize the work that is being done. [Although] to some people we are perhaps too socially minded and to other people we preach too much! There is evidence that we change lives. That is what we want. That's what we see. And I think that the people who want to be a part of that are glad to support us.

And later he added:

The United Way has a program called Donor's Choice. If you work for a company, you can give to the United Way and designate your gift. Also we have access to a program through the State of Connecticut; it is a reimbursement program, for individuals who are going through a drug and alcohol program like this. They qualify, if they are indigent, for their costs for staying in a program of recovery via a state reimbursement to help them access the service. That has been a great help to us.

The need simply demands innovative response, in search of income sources that are necessary to support social ministries.

Christian Activities Council

I think there were over 40 funding sources last summer. We applied,
and just sent out a raft of proposals to foundations and corporations.

One pastor explained that he approaches fund raising with the biblical
injunctions that he finds in the Scripture for prayer. "Seek and you shall
find; knock and it will be opened to you." As a source of energy, money
never replaces Christian commitment, but without financial resources the
best intentions cannot be sustained.

Develop Partners and Mediators

Networks among churches and faith-based agencies are essential both to strengthen and to protect local ministries. As centers of religious and social life, in most activities congregations tend to stand alone as self-sustaining communities of faith. Few congregations are large enough to marshal sufficient physical, spiritual, and financial resources to carry the load of a social outreach ministry alone. In practice, larger churches with more resources are even more likely to work with other partners and allies in developing community ministry, while smaller congregations seem less inclined to include others in their ministries.

For a ministry to have an impact, sponsoring congregations need some relationship with other organizations in two ways: On a peer level, congregations benefit from partners and allies that are variously involved in the ministry, brining different gifts to a common cause. Partners have contractual commitments in the ministry, and are generally represented on the governing board. Allies may contribute something to the cause without the responsibilities of decision making. Hardware stores can be allies in housing ministries; schools and libraries can be allies in

---

IV.4

RESOURCES FOR DEVELOPING MEDIATORS AND PARTNERS

Fisher, Robert. *Let the People Decide: Neighborhood Organizing in America.* New York: Twayne, 1994.

Harrison, Bennett, and Marcus Weiss. *Networking Across Boundaries: New Directions in Community Based Job Training and Economic Development.* Boston: Economic Development Assistance Consortium, 1998.

Warren, Mark R., and Richard L. Wood. *Faith Based Community Organizing: The State of the Field.* Jericho, N.Y.: Interfaith Funders, 2001.

educational programs. Both partners and allies reassure the sponsoring congregation that it is not alone.

Mediators have a different relationship with faith-based ministries. They serve as an umbrella agency that provides an administrative link between the government funding source and the local ministry (or ministries). Mediators allow faith-based ministries to utilize their best gifts without being overwhelmed by the red tape of management functions and administrative details.

Successful community ministries build incrementally on their current strengths. Faith-based programs know their turf, and they are known by others throughout the community. Trust—personal and institutional—forms the basis for relationships with partners, allies, and mediators. At the center of trust is a clear and common understanding of the work to be done. In the congregations with whom we worked, some ministry leaders and groups defined their task in its simplest terms as the foundation for working with others.

University Park Christian Church

During the first year, we will address the critical issues that must be resolved before an adult day-care facility can be established in our neighborhood: money, location, and management.

Some congregations spelled out the challenge they faced, and looked for additional help to reach these goals. Notice in this description the implied distinctions between partners who share leadership, and allies to whom referrals are made.

St. Boniface Catholic Church

During the implementation year, the core committee in consultation with the partnering groups will put in place the particulars for the project including: securing and readying a facility; writing by-laws, operating procedures, job descriptions, and training manuals; developing programming and a general record-keeping system; recruiting, orienting, and training staff both paid and volunteer; broadening our base of partnering groups in the community; engaging in fund raising by asking individuals and groups for money and submitting grants to appropriate funding sources as well as developing a suitable financial record-keeping system; and overseeing a study of the area homeless and the availability of low-cost housing in Lafayette County.

The challenge is to expand your vision with new resources, without reducing your congregation's sense of ownership and commitment to the ministry program. These working relationships allow faith communities to mobilize and sustain an indigenous program through a network of connections that can reach their communities.

Mediating institutions are filling a crucial role for congregations that are the point-of-service delivery. Mediating agencies enhance congregational abilities in many ways, such as (1) develop paid staff and volunteers through in-service training; (2) find diverse revenue streams from the faith communities themselves and from government, business, and philanthropy; (3) coach board members in issues of vision, governance, and finance; (4) address legal matters of incorporation, contract, copyright, insurance, etc.; and (5) enable a process of strategic planning and program evaluation. In essence, mediators directly or by oversight lift the burden of administration from the congregation, thus liberating congregations to spend their energies in areas of greatest strength—ministry.

But congregations must be aware that all such relationships come at a price. They complicate decision making, even as they broaden horizons and resources. You may recognize the feelings behind this experience:

Hope Presbyterian Church
We assume that the four groups [working together] with differing traditions and motivations, yet similar visions, will be able to amicably address policy decisions and arrive at consensus. We are still struggling with how much control authority Hope Church should rightfully expect to exercise.

Given the need and the fear, it is not surprising that congregations find mediators, partners, and allies from contacts they make in their routines of ministry. You can look for help among people you trust and institutions that share your commitments. We have identified five areas where congregations have found common ground and built strong ministries. These are not mutually exclusive, since building social ministry is a pragmatic effort toward "whatever works for you." For partners, allies and mediators, congregations have turned to several existing relationships: (1) denominational connections, (2) affinity groups, (3) social agencies, (4) community-action coalitions, and (5) ad hoc assemblies.

DENOMINATIONAL CONNECTIONS

The first inclination of many congregations is to find peer partners from others like themselves to share with them in ministry. One pastor caught this spirit in the simplicity of his comment:

Sweet Holy Spirit Baptist Church
We want to work with other churches. . . .

Many congregations belong to denominations that they approach for help in developing social ministries. Even independent congregations have Sunday school organizations, theological school networks, and similar religious associations such as those loosely related to the National Association of Evangelicals. These church organizations can give identity, information, technical skill, and sometimes substantial financial support. Thus it seemed natural for this Catholic church to use its denominational network to find its partners from among its suburban sister congregations.

St. Michael's Catholic Church
The tutoring program was started with the Community Renewal Team, and we have worked in conjunction with suburban parishes, which supply us with materials for the kids, notebooks, and nutritious snacks, that kind of thing—plus monies.

Denominational connections offer a combination of volunteers, funding, expertise, and contacts with congregations locally and across the country, which share common perceptions, interests, and faith commitments. A generation ago they might have been the primary resource for congregations in community ministries. No longer.

AFFINITY GROUPS

Congregations are more likely to reach out to others in different denominations than to remain limited by their own structures. In the massive data from many different denominations in the FACT study, 29 percent of the congregations found partners from within their own denomination, while 38 percent crossed denominational lines to develop partners in outreach ministries. Equally interesting, congregations were even more likely to worship together as to work together in social ministries (see fig. 14). Thus this report from Canton is representative of many associations that begin in partnerships and mature into mediating agencies.

Figure 14.
Cross-Denominational Partners for Social Ministry and for Worship

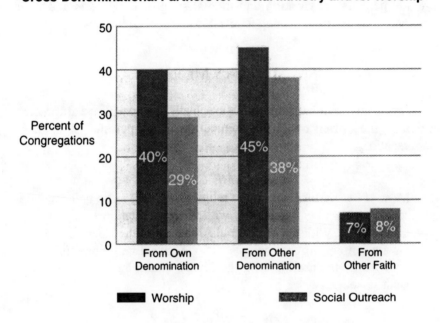

St. Mary's Catholic Church, Canton
St. Mary's Catholic Church and the First Congregational UCC of Canton, IL (known hereafter as the partnering churches) have chosen to call their project Christian Service Program. . . . Pastors of the partnering churches, or their designated representatives, will be members of the Advisory Council. Other Advisory members . . . would include persons with specialized knowledge in areas such as: legal, fund-raising, grant-writing, public relations, and human resources. Standing committees will be formed for Fund-Raising, Building Management, Publicity, Program Administration, Advocacy, and Human Resources. Special committees will be appointed as needed. . . . Each member church and its congregation

are expected to provide leadership, manpower, and financial support on specific needs and for annual operating expenses.

Most congregations develop organizational ties with the informal "affinity groups" of congregations they know well. They find more trust and social compatibility among these associations based on a common ground, real and spiritual, such as geography, culture, and ethnicity. These groups typically provide personal networking and mutual support for pastors and their congregations by strengthening fellowship and social relations.

SOCIAL AGENCY MEDIATORS

Most frequently, faith-based ministries eventually link up with social agencies, although they often make the connection in cooperation with other congregations.

Bethel AME Church
Most of our partners are in the religious arena. . . . Some of the secular groups that we partner with, their motivation is slightly different. . . . With the Ministerial Alliance and the Board of Ed, we are forming some programs. . . . We have a very powerful, a very strong partnership with the Jewish community, especially Beth Israel.

St. Peter's Catholic Church
We have a food pantry, which is supplied mostly by suburban Catholic churches, that are donating food to us. We are also a member of Foodshare, Inc., so if we need to, we buy extra food. And that is distributed to the people once a month—free.

As faith-based ministries increase in complexity and responsibility, congregational leaders shift their emphasis from using ties with other religious groups to building program alliances with nonprofit social agencies. Typically these agencies are run by professional leaders, but their programs make use extensively of volunteers recruited from constituent congregations. In a wide variety of forms, they become "managing mediators," providing the kind of technical leadership that relieves congregations of administrative burdens.

Unitarian Society of Hartford

We wanted to find a big project, and we started to educate ourselves and realized that we couldn't do this by ourselves. No more of this "Lady Bountiful" stuff; we needed to work in partnership with the community. . . . The congregation about 4-5 years ago decided that they were not doing enough in Hartford and . . . so we interviewed 18 agencies of the city and chose one as the agency that we wanted to partner with. For our focus we really tried to focus on that agency as a way to get people working together on a common goal.

In organizing to share the tasks, you need more help from realists than from romantics. In this example the leaders define how each partner contributes to the whole:

Irvington United Methodist Church

The partners will be an integral part of the Center organizational structure. . . . Seats given to the Partners on the Board of Directors will insure continuity and ongoing involvement. Each Partner must secure the full cooperative backing from their organization in writing. A financial commitment will be sought from the Partners in whatever form their organizational structure permits; i.e., financial grant, fund raising, membership, donated equipment, publicity, etc. Partners will hold full Executive Board and Committee Officer and Committee positions. Volunteer staff from the Partners will be recruited, trained, and utilized.

At the same time, agencies gain in the arrangement. By using church volunteers, social agencies can decentralize their work and extend their services into the communities where the congregations are located. The challenge is for the church to own the project, but to get the agency to manage it, as reflected in the inner-city effort to create a neighborhood facility.

St. Boniface Catholic Church

Our plan is to acquire an economically efficient facility that can accommodate both individuals and families in a safe and secure environment until these persons can find normal living arrangements. . . . As we currently envision this project, the services of the Transitional Housing Center would include meals, transportation, housing search and placement, and recreational activities. Referrals [to related agencies] will be made for: financial assistance, child care, substance abuse, physical or emotional abuse, pastoral or long-term counseling, job readiness and literacy skills, job training, budget and money management counseling, housekeeping skills, parenting skills, hygiene and nutrition education, and health assessment screening, including necessary health care.

COMMUNITY ACTION COALITIONS

Beyond their associations with existing faith-based social agencies, many congregations develop strong partners, allies, and self-mediating organizations in community action coalitions. These advocacy groups find their roots in networks of faith-based groups, but also may incorporate unions, schools (or parent-teacher groups), neighborhood associations, and other civic bodies that share their commitments to advocate for justice and correct the causes of social ills.

Typically these groups are themselves mediating organizations that hire professional organizers, who may have contracts with national community-action networks. They develop a strong spirit of trust among the participating pastors, members, and congregations that generates important social capital for defining the action and sustaining the engagement. These two examples are drawn from significantly different settings (Lacon is a small town, One Chane is located in a center city area) with common strategies for involving coalitions of congregations and community groups in influencing public policy and allocation of resources.

Immaculate Conception Catholic Church
We proposed that the Lacon Community Center be a membership-based organization, meaning that the members will direct the organization through a board of directors. . . . A membership-based organization is one that gets its power and direction through the grassroots. It has the most potential for empowering members and those involved, through education, experience, organizing, and advocacy. We do not want to start a senior citizen center that only provides services and does not empower seniors or community members.

One Chane, Inc.
When we first started, we decided that church-based organizing was the best way to go. Every incident we have ever dealt with, we find a local church which has the most impact within the targeted area, and get them involved right away, and we launch from there.

AD HOC ASSEMBLIES

Finally, ad hoc groups emerge in response to community crises or recognized need. Based on their common perception of an issue, their endurance depends upon the ability of initial leadership to develop administrative infrastructure that will sustain the broad coalitional character of their composition. As indigenous, value-based institutions, congregations are essential to these ad hoc coalitions. But these ad hoc groups can include a unique mixture of business and labor, of government and private sector, of educational and philanthropic institutions—united in a common cause.

In rural areas and smaller towns where the leaders of social, financial, political, and religious organizations are well known to each other, we often find that apparently different participants are often the same people representing separate aspects of their commercial, social, and religious lives. In the following rural partnership, the number of people involved was less than the number of organizations listed—some individuals simply wore two hats:

First Baptist Church
To date we have commitments for support and volunteers from the Burnettsville Town Board, Burnettsville Community Board, Washington Township Trustee, Burnettsville State Bank, Burnettsville Senior Citizens Club, and the Burnettsville Mennonite Fellowship. We expect to work closely with them in operation and fund raising.

Sometimes such ad hoc coalitions simply emerge from the personal connections of the leaders, even in the complexity of city life. Note how the entrepreneurial director of this agency uses her former professional life as a natural extension of her program support in this soup kitchen/job-training program:

Loaves and Fishes, Inc.
A lot of things I have been able to pull together are because of my business contacts. In cooperation with other people—well, networking is the name of the game . . .

Growing out of a disturbing community crisis, congregations can generate new and amazing initiatives in ministry ad hoc, unrestrained by the absence of an existing structure to maintain it:

Asylum Hill Congregational Church
This is a sort of entrepreneurial church, in that if a layperson comes and says, "I have an idea," we'll say, "We'll get a group together and see if we can make it work."

This kind of pragmatic ad-hocracy gains momentum when it catches the spark of community concern around a particular problem or issue, receiving its initial energy boost from that crisis and the passion of local leaders. Its endurance as faith-based ministry depends heavily upon the ability of initial leadership to develop and shift the administrative work beyond pastoral leadership to a mediating organization that can implement and sustain the ministry. "Pastors alone are ill-equipped for this aspect of ministry," concluded H. Dean Trulear in his overview of faith-based ministries. In particular he cited a well-known example combining social work professionals with committed clergy:[3]

The work of the Ten Point Coalitions in a variety of cities across the country exemplify such an initiative. These coalitions consist of congregations that focus specifically on juvenile violence reduction, and reclaiming high risk youth. Galvanized by the crisis of juvenile violence, these congregations found the need to come together and pool their resources in order to develop a seamless web of services for youth. They also realized the need for centralized staff to handle issues such as fund raising, facilitating cooperation between law enforcement, juvenile justice, community organizations, and the congregations. Since they are task based, their missions are specific; they possess significant ability to be productive and efficient in the development and implementation of programs.

Big Step 4

Enhance Spiritual Experiences

The number of outreach ministries is amazing, when you count the cost! Given that community ministries require such effort and a constant infusion of resources and negotiation among partners with mediators, why do so many congregations keep on doing it? Because it is scriptural and it is needed, as we have noted several times. But more, they do it because touching the lives of others is spiritually satisfying in ways that are different from worship and prayer, different from fellowship and study. Social ministries carry their own uniquely transforming power to all who participate in these communities of the Spirit.

As the riptides of feeling from the September 11, 2001, emergency settle into the psyche of the nation, more people are willing to volunteer for mundane roles in caring ministries. Significant relationships occur among volunteers, as well as with clients and other participants of community ministries. Little things make a difference. The act of touching another person means being touched in return, and in that physical contact participants feel spiritually nurtured.

Further, larger purposes for these ministries are now more clearly in view, even if, in honesty, they seem more complex and difficult to achieve. Leaders know they can make a difference in the lives of individuals, and, by

---

IV.5
RESOURCES FOR
SUSTAINING YOUR SPIRITUAL ENERGY

Gunderson, Gary. *Deeply Woven Roots: Improving the Quality of Life in Your Community.* Minneapolis: Fortress, 1997.

Loeb, Paul Rogat. *Soul of a Citizen: Living with Conviction in a Cynical Time.* New York: St. Martin's Griffin, 1999.

extension, congregations can accept larger challenges of making a difference in their communities. Congregations are the safety net for individuals in crises. In many communities, they are the steeple or dome that symbolizes refuge from the worst, as well as the hope that the world can be a better place, individually and in community. That spark of hope keeps community ministries alive in difficult times, and the warmth of that hope enables us to feel fleeting moments of success.

Beyond their communities, congregations take an even longer view by making a difference in the next generation. A review of the kinds of ministries that congregations accept reflects their commitment to education and nurture for children, and willingness to work with prison and immigrant ministries—long-term investments that can only be sustained by a vision for a better world, someday.

TRANSLATING DIVERSITY INTO ENERGY

In the shock of September 11 and the shadow of charitable-choice legislation, we live with a new climate in community ministries across the country. It is characterized by the integrity of faith and action, by the authenticity that allows participants to express openly their beliefs without demanding conformity. These are comfortable expressions of spirituality that accompany many social ministries—as if the two are twin expressions of one common impulse to embrace both God and neighbor, "naturally."

All the material of this study points to a strong religious commitment to "both/and," not "either/or." We have:

- *both* particular faith expressions (Christian, Jewish, Muslim) and interfaith coalitions working together for common causes;
- *both* racial solidarity and cultural diversity (in the same ministry);
- both commitment to individuals (compassion) and intervention toward transformation (justice);
- *both* spiritual nurture and community ministry, both evangelism and social action;
- *both* ministries that are located in urban areas and cross-cultural flow of volunteers from suburban congregations;
- *both* church and state, both faith-based programs and government funds in common ministry.

These liaisons are not based on eliminating the differences, or on "standing in the middle of the bridge." Rather the common commitments in ministry provide a spiritual bridge that makes the connection possible. For most there is a primary emphasis on making the faith visible "in the streets."

Divine Light Baptist Church

What we have found by adopting a street is being visible in the community. People begin to look at the church in a more positive view because when you think that you are just inside and don't care about people on the outside. So in order to do that, to fight that mindset, you have to be visible. That's the object. So we try to revitalize and transform this neighborhood. That is what church is all about.

Other people report a long-term commitment to be here as long as it takes, until the children of next generation comes into their own:

Loaves and Fishes, Inc.

Welfare reform, I think, will probably have very little positive effect on the adults who are involved in it, because most of them are going through such a difficult time. . . . I hope that their kids will benefit by that whole sense of going to work, a good attitude toward work—and I think that is where Welfare to Work is going to make a difference, and I think that is wonderful. But I think this generation is pretty much lost to a real change for the better.

Still others suggest a basic hope in and through congregations, even if, at this moment in history, they cannot be sure exactly how to make it happen.

Center City Churches

The difference that I see is this: It used to be that public assistance was the permanent system and church intervention . . . was the temporary fix, because the state welfare was there. Now we have turned that on its ear. We have said that welfare is the temporary fix, the short-term kind of a solution. So we don't know what the other permanent one is going to be. Churches and nonprofit agencies [must] . . . figure out new ways to work with these people.

Agency leaders admit a significant satisfaction in helping congregational members discover the power of their own faith-in-action as they are touched in the act of touching others.

Covenant to Care
The clergy and the congregation members have often said, "This has revitalized us!" or "This has brought a new perspective to our outreach ministry." That is wonderful. That is what we intended to do. It is extremely rewarding . . . a shot in the arm in connecting their faith to the purposes that they felt were very important. . . . The other piece is the satisfaction of gaining the entry into the congregation to help them realize that the children are suffering, and . . . there are things they can do to alleviate that.

For some, energy comes in the deep satisfaction of seeing the whole culture of the congregation transformed, and being able to pass that along to new members who join the ministry.

Unitarian Society of Hartford
I think that it helps us come together. . . . You might expect that a year or two after something like this that people would be tired. Rather it has grown. . . . It has actually become so much a part of the fabric of the congregation that new members see that as a benefit.

For some spiritual satisfaction rests in the reaffirmation of relationships (divine and human), the transforming quality in divine activity, and the need for focus in our busy lives.

Center City Churches, Inc.
[Three new priorities]: One is the importance of volunteers, recognizing that their sense of relationship is critical to what we do; second, we are a faith-based organization and we want to affirm that in ways that change people's lives, without proselytizing; and third is we want to go deeper rather than broader.

In a surprisingly ecumenical embrace, one leader reverses the common notion that churches depend on government funding, and explains why the energy flows in the other direction, and has for a long time.

Glory Chapel International Cathedral/Youth Challenge
But the need is greater than our ability to meet the need. We know that we are not able to do it alone. We are not the only church or residential center in Hartford. There are many churches and other good works, thank God. Really the state is counting on the church—they might not want to acknowledge that they do. But the church has always been there. There are some regulations about receiving money, but something has happened to the people we work with. I can't just ignore that or act like it didn't happen, or act like it is attributable to something else because that would be to take away the heartbeat of the motivation.

These spiritual affirmations fit comfortably with the motives that first proposed charitable choice for faith-based ministries. From these examples we might doubt if government funding works equally well for everyone, for "both large and small" congregations, as the president proposed. But the legislation pushes all congregations to ask the right questions, to reconsider their priorities, and to imagine new possibilities. Despite the complications and limitations of social ministries in conditions of this post-9/11 world, these faith-based programs would appear to be remarkably effective and spiritually satisfying for those who are moved to participate.

Big Steps Toward Social Ministry

Big Step 1: Establish Your Ministry Niche (pp. 142-149)

We have found a niche where our social ministry can make a difference, and considered pros and cons of receiving publish funding.
Date: _____   Assigned to:_____

We have decided to explore further possibilities for public funding.
Date: _____   Assigned to:_____

Big Step 2: Employ Staff and Raise Money (pp. 150-158)

We have investigated the need to hire (or expand) paid staff.
Date: _____   Assigned to:_____

We have made a decision on employing full-time or part-time staff.
Date: _____   Assigned to: _____

We have assigned a study of fund-raising possibilities.
Date: _____   Assigned to: _____

We have a fund-raising plan approved and in place.
Date: _____   Assigned to: _____

Big Step 3: Develop Partners and Mediators (pp. 159-168)

We have decided whether to remain on our own or to seek partners and allies with whom to share our ministry.
Date: _____   Assigned to: _____

We have identified and contacted potential partners for our ministry.
Date: _____   Assigned to: _____

We have identified a social agency, coalition or other umbrella organization that will help us manage our ministry.
Date: _____   Assigned to: _____

Big Step 4: Enhance Spiritual Experiences (pp. 169-173)

We have integrated the community ministry purpose with the congregation's spiritual expression..
Date: _____   Assigned to: _____

We have designed a process to encourage and sustain the spiritual growth of all leaders and participants in our ministry.
Date: _____   Assigned to: _____

Mobilizing Your Ministry

Unfortunately, I have discovered that congregational leadership committees for social ministry often get bogged down, and these moments of struggle and indecision occur at predictable places. I list seven areas where I have commonly seen problems occur—not to suggest that you can avoid them altogether, but to offer solace and suggestions when you find yourselves in these quandaries as you move to develop or expand your ministry.

First, leadership is basic to developing your ministry. But finding the "one right leader" is rarely enough. Rather, as your ministry matures, different people must step forward to take those responsibilities for which they seem best suited. Strength lies more in the discovery and succession of leadership than in the strength of the initial group. A basic job of all leaders is to find and prepare their replacements.

Second, clergy support is crucial to the development of community ministry, but the importance and the style of pastoral leadership vary greatly, depending on cultural and denominational traditions and the particular people involved. Your social-concerns committee can do well, sometimes even better, without hands-on clergy leadership, but not without the pastor's (or rabbi's or imam's) vocal, public support.

Third, broad participation is the backbone of strong ministry. Although I endorse the need for a small, committed core committee, both the knowledge and the work of ministry must be shared with a larger group far beyond the immediate leaders. I noted many examples of the importance of frequent project interpretation and a creative use of numerous volunteers. Bluntly said, in my experience the absence of broad participation and support is the single most frequent cause of project failure.

Fourth, since planning is a weakness of many efforts toward ministry, I encourage core groups to plan in a way that is appropriate to your task, leadership, and cultural context. Throughout my experience I see a wide variety of organizing styles that work, but a "nonplanning style" never helps. Clarity of goals helps to keep the committee going in the face of interesting distractions and the inevitable moments of discouragement and despair. Planning specific steps helps members to know what each should be doing next. Whatever the style, successful planning generally has committed leaders, clear goals, and specific steps—and then makes the most of whatever happens.

Fifth, the practice of pragmatism—making the most of whatever happens—is both an organizational strategy and a religious conviction. The religious conviction assumes that since God can use this and every moment, there must be something in this experience (anticipated or unexpected, wonderful or "disastrous") that God will help you deal with as you work toward your goal. Pragmatism turns the belief into action. Most social ministries achieve some of their basic goals, but most do it differently from the way they originally anticipated. The gift is knowing when to hang on to your initial vision and when to amend the particulars to achieve your larger goals.

Sixth, mobilize congregational identity in support of social ministry. Embedded in the energy of the memory of virtually every congregation are the scriptural precedents, canonic and creedal statements, stories of events, and particular people that can be mobilized as forerunners and rationale for your ministries of compassion and justice. Some core committees emphasize how new the ministry appears, failing to use the strength of local history and the great tradition of their faith. Some committees take on too much too fast, failing to inform and integrate their natural allies in the present composition of the congregation. Regardless of present practices, every congregation has a reservoir of memories and models on which to build programs of social ministry. They may be new, but rooted in the past. They may be destined to grow like the oak, but they begin like an acorn, with the strength of the past encoded within.

Seventh, claim your spiritual gift of ministry. When seen as a burden laid on us for the sake of others or as an obligation, social ministries can exhaust and burn out some strong and loving people. But faith-based ministries can generate spiritual gifts that energize staff, invigorate volunteers, and enliven congregations in the act of reaching out to others. It happens when you recognize your resources and your limits and do not try to do it all alone. Some of your additional help will come from partners and allies in your community. Mediators will help when they share their expertise, wider experience, and additional resources. Beyond the human and physical resources, at times you must simply back off—"let go and let God"—in a quiet moment, or a worship event, or a weekend retreat or whatever seems (super-)natural to you. Community ministry must remain a spiritual gift, and when that ceases, perhaps it's time to back off and begin again.

Beginning with the creative energy of our God, an awareness of some of the needs of your community, and the acts of compassion and justice called forth by our faith traditions, you have all the resources necessary for social ministry in your community.

Introduction

1. Sections of this chapter have been abridged from Carl S. Dudley, "Faith-Based Community Ministries in a 9-11 World," in *September 11, 2001: A Historical, Theological and Social Critique* (Oxford, England: Oneworld Publications, 2002); used by permission.

2. Faith Communities Today (FACT) includes 14,301 congregations from 41 denominational and faith communities; see Carl S. Dudley and David A Roozen, *Faith Communities Today (FACT): A Report on Religion in the United States Today* (Hartford: Hartford Institute for Religion Research, Hartford Seminary, 2001), on line at *www.fact.hartsem.edu.*

3. Carolyn Said, "Foundations launch campaign to support safety net charities," *San Francisco Chronicle,* Dec. 5, 2001, from Web site *www.sfgate.com.*

4. From "Philanthropy Notes" in *Foundation Watch* (Dec. 2001), Washington, D.C.: Capital Research Center, *www.capitalresearch.org.*

5. From "The Mosque in America: A National Portrait," using data gathered in cooperation with Faith Communities Today study (above), published in *A Report from the Mosque Study Project* (Washington, D.C.: Council on American-Islamic Relations, April 2001). On line at *www.cair-net.org*

6. Quotes from congregations and agencies from Carl S. Dudley, *Welfare, Faith-Based Ministries, and Charitable Choice* (Hartford: Hartford Institute for Religion Research, for Program for Non-Profit Organizations, Yale University, March 2001). On line at *www.hirr.hartsem.edu.* Also from Carl S. Dudley, *Basic Steps toward Community Ministries* (Washington: Alban Institute, 1991) and *Next Steps in Community Ministry* (Bethesda: Alban Institute, 1996), and from Carl

S. Dudley and Sally A. Johnson, *Energizing the Congregation: Images That Shape Your Church's Ministry (Louisville: Westminster John Knox, 1993).*

Part IV
1. Laurie Goodstein, "A Nation Challenged: Religion; As Attacks' Impact Recedes, A Return to Religion as Usual," *New York Times*, Nov. 26, 2001, *www.nytimes.qpass.com/qpass-archives.*

2. Bob Wineberg, "The Spirit of Charitable Choice" (Greensboro, N.C.: School of Social Work, University of North Carolina, 1999). Published as an occasional paper.

3. Harold Dean Trulear, "Faith-Based Institutions and High-Risk Youth" (Philadelphia: Public/Private Ventures, Field Report Series, spring 2000). Dean Trulear's views have strongly influenced this section.

Appendix D
1. Adapted from Dudley and Johnson, *Energizing the Congregation.*

Topical Index of Published Resources

Brief Descriptions of Congregations and Faith-Based Ministries

I. Brief descriptions of churches, agencies, and faith-based ministries in Indiana and Illinois participating in the *Church and Community Project, 1987–1996:*

Avondale Presbyterian Church, in a culturally diversified section of Chicago, developed TAP, The Afterschool Program, to stimulate primary-school children.

Community Covenant Church of Calumet Park, Illinois, is located in a racially changing middle-class Chicago suburb. It began an Educational Resource Center to offer GED (General Educational Development) classes and tutoring for teens and young adults in the neighborhood.

Community United Church of Christ is one of the oldest congregations in the Chicago bedroom community of Morton, Illinois. Through Daybreak, Inc., this church and seven others offer day care for the frail elderly.

Cornell Baptist Church meets in a large renovated home in a racially mixed community near a major university in Chicago. The small congregation actively supports STRIVE as a Christian ministry of tutoring and enrichment activities for elementary school children.

Deer Creek Presbyterian Church, with its manse, stands alone in the fields. With its nearest neighbor, Faith Lutheran Church, the Presbyterian congregation built a community center for social, educational, and cultural events.

Douglas Park Covenant Church combines an older Swedish-heritage congregation with the younger Iglesia del Pacto Evangélica de Douglas Park (total 200 membership). The church developed a Family Education Center, which offers after-school tutoring, activities, and parenting education.

Edwin Ray United Methodist Church and two other small United Methodist congregations (each under 100 members) work for community renewal through better housing in their low-income community, using a "sweat equity" basis to purchase and provide care for others.

First Baptist Church of Burnettsville, Indiana (population 500), sponsors the Burnettsville Community Youth Center in the recently renovated gym of an old abandoned school building.

First Meridian Heights Presbyterian Church, with 500 members and a significant endowment, is located in a racially changing area in Indianapolis, Indiana. Along with three neighboring congregations, the church hired a community organizer worker for programs in substance-abuse prevention, nutrition, life skills, and mediation training for at-risk youth, particularly gang members.

First Presbyterian Church, Canton, is a congregation of about 400 in a central Illinois town. Working with a neighboring Wesleyan Methodist church, they developed a resource exchange program through which town residents help meet each other's needs.

Fisher United Methodist Church, located in a small Illinois town, was strongly influenced by changing family patterns that left children unattended in the afternoons. In response the church began the Fisher Key Club, offering educational enrichment for "latchkey" children.

Good News Community Church/Iglesia Buenas Nuevas is a small congregation composed of Anglos, Latinos, and African Americans in a low-income, racially mixed neighborhood of Chicago. It provides safe space for youth in educational, social, and enrichment activities.

Hope Presbyterian Church has a small (200) but well-educated membership in Springfield, Illinois. The congregation embraced a partnership of three community agencies to serve infants, elders, and families in crisis with active programs that use the new building all day, every day.

Immaculate Conception Catholic Church (300) and three mainline Protestant congregations in the river town of Lacon, Illinois, constructed a facility to provide daily meals, socializing, and advocacy for elderly citizens; a nursery school; teen dances; 4H; and other community groups.

Immanuel Lutheran Church, with its Swedish Lutheran immigrant heritage, sponsors employment training and English classes for Indochinese immigrants. Its partner Lutheran Chinese Christian Church extends the ministry into the mini-Chinatown of restaurants, shops, and professional services.

Irvington United Methodist Church, a large (1,000) but aging congregation in a culturally diverse community of Indianapolis, offers a variety of services and social opportunities for isolated elderly throughout the community.

Lafayette Church of the Brethren (in Indiana) maintains a strong program that provides mediators for a reconciliation center involving court offenders and their victims and for settling other community disputes.

Leet Memorial United Methodist Church and Boyd's Grove United Methodist Church (450 members combined), in a small agricultural town, train youth in job skills through supervised home maintenance and repair services for senior citizens in the community.

Manchester Church of the Brethren, the flagship church (750 members) for the large German pietist group in Manchester, Indiana, trains elementary children as mediators in conflicts among their peers, and trains adults in skills to mediate community disputes.

Martin Temple African Methodist Episcopal Zion Church, a thriving, middle-class congregation of about 500 members, hopes to prevent school dropout by providing academic and cultural enrichment for elementary-school children.

Millard Congregational Church, United Church of Christ/Iglesia Evangélica Unida de Cristo, a small congregation on Chicago's West Side, developed a pre-college program to prepare neighborhood teens for entrance examinations and college-level work.

North United Methodist Church (1,200 members), in a classic neo-gothic structure in Indianapolis, developed a program with educational, economic, social, and mentoring components.

Ridge Lutheran Church (350 members) sponsors HANDS, through which representatives from the deaf, hearing-impaired, and hearing communities advocate for the needs of the deaf and hearing-impaired.

Riverside Park United Methodist Church (75 members), located in an economically diverse African-American neighborhood in Indianapolis, offers nourishment, tutoring, and social activities to elementary-age children after school.

St. Boniface Catholic Church, an old German congregation (800) in downtown Lafayette, Indiana, provides transitional housing for low-income families, and social services and advocacy for community housing needs.

St. Joan of Arc Catholic Church, which has about 1,000 families in a racially mixed area of Indianapolis, sponsors educational and recreational opportunities for youth, along with mentoring for personal development.

St. Luke's United Methodist Church, an active congregation (750 members) with many management and supervisory personnel from the automotive industry of Kokomo, Indiana, offers tutoring to nonreading adults, with a goal of improved employability.

St. Mary's Catholic Church, Alexandria, a modest parish (500 families) in Alexandria, Indiana, a once-thriving industrial town that has fallen on hard times, offers parenting education and day care or home care for at-risk children in families under stress.

St. Mary's Catholic Church, Canton, is a blue-collar congregation in Canton, Illinois. Along with the neighboring First Congregational United Church of Christ, it provides assistance with health-insurance claims for elderly residents.

St. Mary's Catholic Church, Indianapolis, developed the Hispanic Wholistic Education Center to reduce the dropout rate among Hispanic students at a local vocational high school and to encourage more Hispanic youth to enroll in higher education.

South Chicago Evangelical Covenant Church, with a handful of faithful families drawn from a Chicago neighborhood of old steel mills and immigrant families, sponsors transitional housing for abused women and their children in a program called WellSpring House.

Sweet Holy Spirit Baptist Church (about 2,000 and growing) offers tutoring and enrichment for grammar-school children from two neighborhood schools, as well as food and clothing distribution, counseling, GED classes, and programs for the elderly.

University Park Christian Church, together with three neighboring congregations in Indianapolis, offers adult day health care and in-home respite care for dependent elderly in association with Catholic Charities, and an annual symposium on elderly health-care issues.

Washburn Christian Church, with only 150 members, has tried to instill a new sense of community pride through a variety of efforts, from printing a brochure to promoting the construction of a common facility.

Washington Street Presbyterian Church (100 members) is assisting low-income homeowners to rehabilitate their substandard homes and join their voices with others in a network for citywide advocacy on housing concerns in Indianapolis.

West Park Christian Church (50 members), in a low-income area of Anglo families in Indianapolis, nurtures personal and social growth by providing comfortable drop-in space for pre-teens through high-school-aged youth.

West Street Christian Church, the largest Protestant church (about 900 members) in the agricultural support community of Tipton, Indiana, has joined with six other churches to provide direct assistance to low-income families, along with counseling, referrals, and advocacy.

Westminster Presbyterian Church, Peoria, Illinois, a substantial congregation (600 members), sponsors a program for single teenaged mothers, enabling young mothers to remain in high school by helping them to network with other social agencies.

II. Brief profiles of churches, agencies, and faith-based ministries included in study of *Welfare, Faith-Based Ministries, and Charitable Choice, 1999-2001.*

Asylum Hill Congregational Church, Hartford, Connecticut, is a leadership church drawing from the larger region, with almost 2,000 members. The congregation mixes cultural backgrounds, yet provides volunteers and funding for many faith-based initiatives.

Bethany Lutheran Church, West Hartford, Connecticut, is a suburban congregation of 700 baptized members, actively engaged in a variety of community ministries with strong support from member volunteers.

Bethel African Methodist Episcopal Church, Bloomfield, Connecticut, a congregation of almost 1,000 members that has moved to the suburbs, remains among the most active and outspoken in city and regional affairs, and in community outreach ministries.

Capitol Region Conference of Churches is an ecumenical organization of the Hartford region with 144 member congregations. It provides program and gives voice in issues of conscience and religious concern.

Center City Churches, Hartford, is a consortium of 12 city churches that provides emergency food, youth education, ministries to senior citizens, hospice for AIDS, and other programs with financial and volunteer support from participating congregations.

Christian Activities Council is a city mission sponsored by United Church of Christ that provides mission education, leadership development, and funding for integrated housing developments.

Christian Conference of Connecticut provides an arena for conversation and a forum for speaking on major issues for bishops, church executives, and other senior religious leaders.

Congregation Beth Israel, West Hartford, is a reform synagogue of about 1,250 families (3,000 members) with a strong reputation for leadership in interfaith groups around civic concerns and social ministries.

Covenant to Care is a Hartford regional agency involving 218 congregations with over 1,000 volunteers working with impoverished children.

Divine Light Baptist Church (a pseudonym), Hartford, has about 1,000 participants on a typical Sunday. The congregation emphasizes day care, educational programs, a health clinic, a family resources center, and other ministries.

First Church of Christ in Hartford, UCC, is the oldest church in Hartford (founded 1634), located by the ancient burial ground. Its diverse membership is typically involved in issues and programs to strengthen the city.

Glory Chapel International Cathedral, Hartford, is a cross-cultural, evangelical congregation with a Sunday attendance of 300. It has a particularly strong Youth Challenge group of 200 participants, and an aggressive shelter program for drug rehabilitation.

Hartford Consortium for Jobs is a training and placement agency working in the Hispanic community with funding from city, state, and private sources.

HART (Hartford Areas Rally Together) is the largest community organization in Hartford. It maintains several service programs (such as the HART Community Job Center, also interviewed) and incorporates neighborhood organizations, with a strong voice in decisions throughout the area.

Loaves and Fishes, Inc., Hartford, is an established soup kitchen serving about 200 families. Recently it has expanded to include skills training in cooking, sewing, etc., and job placement for numerous "graduates."

Office of Urban Affairs, Archdiocese of Hartford, generates support and works in behalf of congregational and specialized Catholic ministries.

One Chane, Inc., gets its name from the Clay Hill and North End communities that it represents (CH and NE). This agency has generated significant new and renovated housing, and related economic and social development in the area.

Phillips Metropolitan Christian Methodist Episcopal Church, Hartford, strongly in the black church tradition, has moved from the suburbs to the city to enable its 500 members to become more actively engaged in many expressions of social ministry.

Salvation Army Marshall House is a temporary shelter for Hartford teen agers and families in transition, with a capacity of 40 and a maximum limit of one month—always stretching the limits.

St. John's Episcopal Church, West Hartford, is a stately structure whose 700 members generate more than $50,000 and numerous volunteers for outreach ministries, primarily in education and housing.

St. Michael's Catholic Church, Hartford, has 500 families drawn from a majority of African Americans and a large minority of Hispanics. The parish supports social programs in cooperation with the Salvation Army.

St. Peter's Catholic Church, Hartford, has 2,000 in weekend worship (6,000 registered). The congregation is multicultured with generational waves of immigration, active in political and social concerns.

Westminster Presbyterian Church, West Hartford, with about 350 members, has perhaps 20 to 30 members involved. They work with Habitat for Humanity and other outreach programs that are encouraged by the board of deacons.

Unitarian Society of Hartford has a congregation of 450 pledging units with a major share of its members active in tutoring at Betances and Sanchez schools and other outreach ministries.

United Methodist Church of Hartford is a racially mixed congregation of 300 members that has a history of social ministries such as day care, food pantry, soup kitchen volunteers, and housing for community groups.

Web Links for Community Ministries

Here are Web links for additional resources with *Community Ministries: Proven Steps and New Challenges to Faith-Based Initiatives*. By using ecumenical and interfaith sources, we hope this list will encourage your exploration of these almost unlimited but always changing possibilities. Here are a few suggestions prepared by Dirk J. Hart, who invites e-mail responses to *DirkJHart@aol.com*.

I.1 Resources for Assessing Community Assets
www.nwrel.org/ruraled/ and go to "publications" (a public education site).

I.2 Resources for Community Analysis
Statistics from the latest census are available at
factfinder.census.gov/servlet/BasicFactsServlet (a government site).
www.easidemographics.com/ (a commercial site).

For Canada:
www.statcan.ca/english/ (a government site).

I.3 Resources for Sensitivity to Marginalized Peoples
How one urban church organized to meet the needs of its parish:
www.stjohnsbowdoinst.org/ and go to "urban mission" (an Episcopal site).

I.4 Resources to Identify Intangible Forces
A discussion of various forces at work in substance abuse prevention:
www.ncrel.org/sdrs/ Click on "family and community" and then "Involving the Community in Prevention" (a public education site).

I.5 Resources for Listening in Your Community
Sample questions and activities on how to listen for community health concerns:
www.jhuccp.org/tools/ Click on "activity" and then "gathering information" (a nonreligious university site).

I.6 Resources for Modeling Community Ministries
The Charitable Choice Handbook for Ministry Leaders, by Amy L. Sherman, is available at *downloads.weblogger.com/gems/cpj/ CCHandbook.pdf* (courtesy of the Center for Public Justice, a civic nonprofit organization grounded in a Christian perspective).

II.1 Resources for Understanding Congregations
Resources and articles on congregational life can be found at *www.congregationalresources.org/* (mainline perspective from Alban Institute) and at *www.easumbandy.com/free_resources.htm* (a Christian site not identified with any particular theological bias).

II.2 Resources for Biblical-Theological Foundations
A Roman Catholic perspective: *www.mcauley.acu.edu.au/~yuri/* and click on "Church History and Ecclesiology."

An Orthodox perspective:
www.holy-trinity.org/ecclesiology/

A Wesleyan/Methodist evangelical perspective:
wesley.nnu.edu/theojrnl/21-25/22-08.htm

A classic Reformed perspective:
www.the-highway.com/c_ecclesiology.html

From a mainline perspective:
www.mccormick.edu/urban/vol1no2/page3.htm
On the same page is a link to a theology of community organization.

II.3 Resources for Denominational Histories and Strategies
Some historic creeds and confessions of Christianity can be found at
www.creeds.net/
Also consult your denominational Web site

II.4 Resources for Mobilizing Congregational Stories
"Telling Congregational Stories," by Nancy T. Ammerman, is found at
rra.hartsem.edu/ Click on "Douglasss Lecture" and then "Nancy
Ammerman" (a mainline site).

II.5 Resources from Recording Congregational Stories
Stories from Iowa churches:
www.iaumc.org/ Click on "get involved," then "local church stories"
(a mainline perspective).

**III.1 Resources for Organizing Case Histories from Rural and Urban
Ministries**
Resources from Alban Institute (mainline):
www.congregationalresources.org/ Click on "public ministry," then
"community ministry" and "charitable choice."

A Jewish synagogue perspective on organizing for social ministry:
www.gatherthepeople.org/ Click on "downloads," then "Congregational
Organizer's Primer."

III.2 Resources for Organization Building
An annotated list for nonprofit organization building:
www.internationalbudget.org/ Go to "the resource section" for many
helpful links (for nongovernment service organizations—no particular
religious bias).

III.3 Resources for Finding and Supporting Volunteers
Annotated links for volunteer management:
www.uwex.edu/li/learner/ Go to "non-profit web sites" for many
informative links, including links on volunteer management and fund raising
(for nonprofit organizations, no particular religious bias).

III.4 Resources for Sharing Leadership
A Lutheran experience in New York:
www.elca.org/eteam/resources/missionp11.htm (a mainline Lutheran site).

III.5 Differing Views for Focusing Ministry
A perspective of the National Council of Churches:
www.ncccusa.org/

IV.1 Resources for Faith-Based Ministries
Links to denominations, organizations, and publications:
www.welfareinfo.org/faithbase.asp (no particular religious bias).
www.iwgonline.org/links/bytradition/ (no particular religious bias).

IV.2 Resources for Enlarging Ministries
An example of a cooperative faith-based ministry that uses both staff and volunteers:
www.actionministries.net/services.htm (mainline).

IV.3 Resources for Fund-Raising Trends and Choices
Some links for fund raising:
www.faithbasednetwork.org/ (broadly Christian and nonsectarian).
pugetsoundresources.com/fbinfo.htm (broadly Christian).
tens.org/link.html (mainline and evangelical links).
www.peopleraising.com (on raising self-support; from an evangelical inner-city minister).

IV.4 Resources for Developing Mediators and Partners
www.cpjustice.org/ (a Christian justice perspective).
www.ccda.org/ (a Christian community-development organization with evangelical roots).
www.wco.com/~altaf/altaf.html (a Muslim perspective).
www.jfrej.org/ (a Jewish perspective).

IV.5 Resources for Sustaining Your Spiritual Energy
A thought-provoking article with interesting links:
www.spirithome.com/modern.html (the author is mainline Lutheran).

A Jewish view:
www.gatherthepeople.org/ Then go to "downloads" and click on "Seeding the Vision: The 'Faith-Link' in Congregational Community Organizing."

Summary Questions for Social Context

I. Summary Questions for Social Context

A. General Information about Your Community

1. Describing your community as you know it
   - What are the boundaries of your church/project service area? What are the major institutions in that community?
   - What one social-economic feature in this community (if any) has the greatest impact on a majority of the residents? Docs this have an impact on your congregation, too? If so, how?
   - How would you describe the community to a stranger?

2. Discovering changes and trends. Using the census data and any supplementary data you have found about your community, what were the major changes or trends in this community in the past 10 years in these areas:
   - population growth/decline;
   - population composition (age, race, education, employment, income, household structure), and
   - industry/economic growth/decline?

Using the current data and future projections, are those trends continuing? If not, how are the patterns changing?

3. Applying data and observations
   - What are some visible signs in the community of the trends that you have discerned? (This could include buildings, traffic patterns, people on the streets, etc.)

- Describe the newcomers in the community. Are these people in need and/or people with advantages and resources? In what ways are newcomers similar to or different from long-standing residents?
- Have you discovered any "invisible" people in your community? If so, who are they? Where do they live? What do they do? Why do they remain "invisible"?
- What resources, allies, and potential partners have you found, and how will you follow up with these contacts?

4. Comparing your community with a larger area
- How do the trends that you observed in your community data compare with the data for the larger area?
- How does the economy compare? Are the population changes similar or different? What does that suggest for your ministry?

B. Interviews with Representatives of the Community

Report at least five interviews with a representative sample of community people, including contacts among newcomers and long-standing residents, people in business and political life, someone in planning, and people familiar with the needs of the group or groups that you hope to serve. In your proposed area of service, interview at least one professional leader and at least one person (perhaps several) who might receive your services and participate in your program. To "put flesh" on the census figures, be imaginative in your interviews. For example, you might be able to interview marginalized and "invisible" people you have found in your research. Your data may be extensive, but you need report only the summaries of these contacts in your summary report. For each interview used, give the name of the person contacted, his or her role in the community, and a brief summary of the key comments or insights that your group attained. Note any follow-up expected from your group.

C. Choosing a Preliminary Focus for Ministry

Given what you have learned about your community:
- What is the need area that you hope to address?
- What kind of ministry do you propose to develop?
- How does your proposed ministry address the need?
- What implications do you see for education and advocacy? For empowerment and increased self-sufficiency of the people with whom you seek to serve? For larger issues you might raise?

II. SUMMARY QUESTIONS FOR CONGREGATIONAL IDENTITY

A. Your History and Heritage

1. Your congregation's history
- What is there in the origin (including the name) of your church that relates to your current concern for ministry in your community?
- Give several examples (stories) of social caring in the history of your church.
- Tell about two or three individuals in your church's history who were (or are) "heroes" or "saints" in ministering to others.

2. Your larger faith heritage
- What stories are there in your denomination's history that show a heritage of ministering to social needs?
- What people in your denominational or broader Christian heritage demonstrate the attitude of social caring that you share?
- What statements has your denomination made regarding social needs and responsive ministries?

B. Your Theological Foundations

1. Your biblical and theological bases
Summarize the biblical and theological foundations for your concern for and approach to ministering to people's social needs.

2. Your mission statement
Summarize or quote from your church mission statement (if you have one) as it relates to your proposed ministry involvement.

C. Your Current Profile

1. Learnings from your membership survey
Correlation of congregational identity and social context
- What have you learned from studying identity and context together that has helped you to set directions for your ministry project?
- Given your learnings about your context and identity, and given your survey of possible social ministries, what now seems appropriate as a challenge for your congregation?

2. Congregational process
- What have you learned about subgroups in your church and how they respond (or have responded) to this proposed ministry?
- Given what you've learned, how will you interpret your proposed ministry, and on what basis will you receive approval and support from your congregation?

3. Development of partnerships
- What have you learned from your identity and context about potential partnering groups, especially about your similarities and differences?
- Given your learnings and the project area(s) in which you are interested, (a) who are your actual partners at this time and (b) who are the potential partners whom you intend to contact?

D. Interpreting and Celebrating Your Identity

Using what you have learned from your history, heritage, theology, and membership survey, plan a worship service or other event that celebrates and embodies your congregation's identity as it relates to social ministry.

III. Summary Questions for Organizing Social Ministry

A. Organizational Structure

Identify the projected organizational structure of your ministry project at its launching. Describe how you expect your organizational structure to work as your ministry project "settles in for the long haul." What elements of those outlined above will remain the same? What will change, and how? Issues to be included:

- What will you do in your project, and how will you do it?
- When will you do it? What is your schedule for implementation? Your projected schedule for offering services? (Will you operate daily? weekly? around the clock?)
- What are the partner churches or agencies working with you? How might these change as the ministry becomes established?
- Who will direct and manage the project? What will be your governing group (core committee, board of managers, etc.)?
- What will be that group's relationship to the contract and partnering churches and agencies? to the current core committee? to the managing staff (if any)?

- Who will make policy decisions, and how?
- What participation will there be in your managing and decision-making structures by individuals from among those who are to be served?
- What legal issues or requirements, if any, need to be addressed as you develop the organizational structure for your ministry? How will you learn about those and satisfy them?
- What are your plans for keeping records on the administration of your ministry project?

B. Personnel

Identify the staff you will need, both paid and volunteer, to get your project off the ground. Describe the staff you expect to need to keep your project running over time. What needs and positions will remain constant? What positions will phase out, and what new ones will arise?

Issues to be included:

- What paid staff positions do you expect to use? Describe these roles.
- How will you recruit people to fill those positions?
- Who will supervise the staff?
- What volunteer positions will you have? Describe these roles.
- Who will supervise those volunteers?
- How will you recruit volunteers? In particular, how will you recruit volunteers from the contract and partnering congregations?
- What plans do you have for developing involvement in volunteer or paid staff roles by some of those served?
- What legal issues or requirements, if any, are there that relate to your use of paid or volunteer staff? How will you address those?
- What records will you need to keep related to your paid and volunteer staff? Who will keep those records, and how?

C. Facilities

Identify the facilities, equipment, etc., that you will need when your ministry project opens. Tell how you expect to meet those needs. Describe the facilities you expect to need over the long haul. Will your starting facilities remain adequate? How do you foresee your needs changing, and how do you expect to meet those changing needs?

Issues to be included:

- What space will your ministry project need? Where do you expect to establish it? Will you own the space? Rent it? Share it?
- What will you need to do to adapt that space to your needs? Renovate? Expand? How will you do that? Who will do that? When?
- What furnishings and equipment will you need? Will they be donated or purchased?
- What supplies or materials will you need for operating your project?
- What participation will the contract and partnering churches have in providing for the facilities needs of your ministry project?
- How will any of those who are served become involved in filling the facilities needs of the project?
- What legal issues or requirements will you encounter in providing for the facilities needs of your project (zoning laws, building codes, etc.)? How will you meet those?
- What records related to your facilities will you need to keep? Who will keep those and how?

D. Finances

1. Start-up: Outline your expected financial needs for the startup phase of your ministry project. Tell how the money will be managed. Include a tentative budget.

2. Ongoing Ministry: Outline your projected financial situation for the long term of your project. How do you expect your needs to change? What continuity and what changes do you foresee in your system of financial management?

3. Fund raising: Describe your plans for developing a fund-raising program. Who will be involved? What types of sources might you explore? How do you expect your fund-raising program to change or remain the same over time?

Issues to be included:
- How much money do you expect to need during the start-up phase of your ministry project (the first year)? How much do you expect to need to continue operating in subsequent years?

- What kinds of potential resources for long-term funding have you discovered so far in your community? (You need not name specific sources at this point, unless you have some contacts already established. At this stage you should be exploring types of sources— businesses, foundations, government grants, etc.)
- What resources do you expect the contract and partner congregations to be able to offer to the ongoing support of the project?
- Who will be responsible for fund raising for your project? What committee or group will do it? Will that include members of core committee? Other members of the congregation(s)? Other persons from the community? What individuals have agreed to participate in that group?
- Who will be responsible for managing the financial affairs for your ministry project? What individuals (by name or by position) will handle the funds? To what group(s) will they be accountable for their management?
- What involvement do you expect representatives of those who are served to have in the development and management of resources for your project?
- What legal issues will you need to address related to the financing of your project? How will you go about dealing with them?
- What plans do you have for keeping financial records for your project? Who will be responsible for this record-keeping?

Gleanings from Years with Community Ministry

What I thought when I was younger, in italic.
What I discovered in my efforts, in bold.

—*I thought churches were religious organizations, but*
I found congregations are relational associations that sometimes make decisions.

— *I thought we could think our way into new habits of action, but*
I discovered that we are more likely to act our way into new habits of thinking.

— *I thought that social ministry begins with the clergy, but*
I discovered that after the blessing of the clergy, we need strong lay leadership.

— *I thought we could begin with existing committees for social concerns, but*
I learned to bypass "issue of the month" clubs to find a few people who want action.

— *I thought we had to find strong and proven leaders, but*
I found the best leaders grew strong in faith-grounded anger, frustration, and hope.

— *I thought that congregational leaders had to study the turf to see its problems, but*
They still could not see issues until they believed that ministry is God's will for them.

— *I thought that community analyses would bring issues to light, but*
I found that mapmaking allows members to become re-rooted in the neighborhood.

— *I thought that the congregation's greatest gifts were its location and building, but*
I found that old friends, personal contacts, individual friendships were the treasure.

— *I thought issues were important to define ministry, but*
I found relationships far stronger: "It hurts more when you call them by name."

— *I thought we should look for the "needs we can meet," but*
That creates dependency—better to ask neighbors, "What needs to be changed?"

— *I thought we should plan every step of the ministry, but*
Better to "learn by doing" with the new energy from "inside the problems."

— *I thought we should always push for creative, imaginative new ministries, but*
The strongest ministries had precedents, building on the confidence of the past.

— *I thought that partners and stakeholders were an easy way to expand ministry, but*
I discovered that including stakeholders requires extra effort, but they are worth it.

— *I thought social ministries might compete with churches for scarce resources, but*
Churches that care about community ministries receive more income for all they do.

— *I was educated to think that liberals are social, conservatives are spiritual; but*
Social ministries cross all boundaries of faith, color, class, politics, and the rest.

— *In workshops I learned to develop the right kind of organization, but*
I discovered many styles work well if the leaders fit and they are trusted by others.

— *I thought that innovations like Charitable Choice must be decided "yes" or "no", but*
I discovered that there is more to be learned by carefully exploring all the options.

— *I thought that administration and record-keeping destroyed the spark of ministry, but*
There are bridge people and mediating organizations making management doable.

— *I heard that conflict undermines the unity in congregations and ministries, but*
Conflict can define the issues, intensify group support, and generate real progress.

— *I might think from political reports that all faith-based organizations are alike, but*
Each one is unique in purpose, participants, culture, and organization.

— *I might think from social work articles that all congregations think alike, but*
Each one is unique in mission, size, beliefs, polity, culture, and character.

One way to discover the character of congregational culture is to listen to the stories the members tell about themselves. These five congregational images (below) suggest different self-images and therefore distinct strategies in community ministries.[1]

Members of a **pillar church** tell stories about its role as an anchor in its community, for which it feels a deep civic responsibility. The architecture often reflects this self-image—strong pillars that lift the roof physically and lift the community spiritually. The building may be modest in a small town, or imposing in a neighborhood that expects a prominent architectural posture. Like the building, members see themselves as pillars of the community, good citizens individually and corporately, sharing a pillar mindset of heritage, leadership, facilities, and finances used to strengthen the whole community (1 Pet. 2:9).

People of a **pilgrim church** have rich stories of caring for their own. As distinguished from the pillar's sense of being rooted in place, pilgrim congregations move with their people. Their culture and their Christian faith are woven in a single fabric of their lives. Some older pilgrim congregations have seen waves of immigrants or racial change, embracing new ethnics among the old to share their story. These are Slovaks or Swedes, for example, whose neighborhood now receives Mexicans or Asians. A pilgrimage memory can also include the "stranger" in their midst (Heb. 11:13f.).

Survivor church members tell of the storms they have weathered, taking pride in their survival like the endurance on the cross. Survivor churches live on the edge, always on the verge of being overwhelmed by emergencies. They do not expect to conquer their problems, but they will not give in. They are determined rather than domineering, relentless rather than aggressive. They hang on because "we've made it through worse than this before." Although outsiders may see these churches as "weak," they can be resilient, productive, and loving when leaders learn to make positive use of their orientation to crises (Matt. 7:2f., 1 Cor. 4:12).

Prophet churches have stories of being called to challenge "the world," which may focus on many manifestations of evil from individuals to corporations, from communities to nations. Independent, often entrepreneurial in style, these crusaders are supported by people who share their commitments. Prophetic churches share with survivors a crisis mentality, but the prophetic are active while the survivors are reactive. These high-profile congregations, whether large or small, often have an unusual impact and set the standards for other congregations (Great commandment and commission, Mic. 6:8).

Members of **servant churches** relish remembering their opportunities quietly to help individual people in personal need. These churches are neither threatened like survivors nor assertive like the prophet. Whereas pillars feel responsible for the whole community and pilgrims respond to a particular people, servants see only individuals in need, and they reach out to help them in supportive and pastoral ways by visiting the sick, taking meals to the bereaved, and sending cards to shut-ins. They are not particularly interested in systemic justice, but faithfully provide food, clothing, and other basic needs to their neighbors, living their faith in service (Mark 9:35, Acts 2:45).

Organizers can mobilize the energy of congregations in ways that honor and utilize their unique self-images.